Equitable School Improvement

Equitable School Improvement

The Critical Need for the Human Side of Change

Rydell Harrison
Isobel Stevenson

TEACHERS COLLEGE PRESS

TEACHERS COLLEGE | COLUMBIA UNIVERSITY

NEW YORK AND LONDON

Published by Teachers College Press,® 1234 Amsterdam Avenue, New York, NY 10027

Copyright © 2024 by Teachers College, Columbia University

Front cover fingerprint texture by Conall via Flickr Creative Commons.

Library of Congress Cataloging-in-Publication Data is available at loc.gov

ISBN 978-0-8077-6958-4 (paper)
ISBN 978-0-8077-6959-1 (hardcover)
ISBN 978-0-8077-8233-0 (ebook)

Printed on acid-free paper
Manufactured in the United States of America

Contents

Preface   ix

Acknowledgments   xv

1. **Iterative Justice**   1

    Why Read This Book?   1

    Mental Models and Institutional Logics   6

    Improving Together   8

    What Do We Mean by Equity, and Why Do We Want It?   9

    Why Improvement Science and Equity Have More in
        Common Than You Might Think   12

    Values That Run Through This Book   16

2. **Centering the Experiences of Students**   18

    Student Centered Versus Centering Students   21

    Belonging and Identity   23

    Marginalized Group Identity   26

    Social Homelessness   29

    Empathy and Empathy Interviews   33

    Focus Groups   35

    At Your Desk or in the Halls   37

3   **Dispositions of the Liberatory Improver**   38

    Background on Dispositions   40

    Dispositions in Improvement Science   42

Dispositions of Equity Leaders in Education   44

Dispositions of Liberatory Improvers   45

At Your Desk or in the Halls   51

4. **The Adjacent Possible**   **53**

Limitations of Traditional Mental Models   55

Leveraging the Adjacent Possible   59

At Your Desk or in the Halls   66

5. **Beliefs About Change and About People**   **69**

Attribution   71

Defensive Routines   73

Bias and Psychological Distance   75

Mindsets   77

Self-Efficacy and Stereotype Threat   80

Identity   81

Motivation   82

Goals and Accountability   83

Psychological Safety   85

At Your Desk or in the Halls   85

6. **Dismantling Traditional Power Structures**   **87**

Traditional Power Structures   88

Rationalization of Power   91

Power and the Perception of Rightness   92

Infantilization and Blame   93

Interrogating the Status Quo   95

Renegotiating Power   96

Embracing Transformative Change   98

Time as a Tool of Power   99

Liberatory Power Sharing   100

At Your Desk or in the Halls   105

7. Broadening Our Concept of Data   **107**

   Data Contaminated by History   108

   A Test-Based Theory of Action   109

   Poor Assumptions and Unintended Consequences   112

   Reconfiguring Data Teams to Make Better Use of Data
      and Empower Teachers   117

   A Word on Equity Audits   122

   At Your Desk or in the Halls   123

8. The Absolute Necessity of Conversation   **124**

   Why Conversations About Race Are So Difficult   125

   The Privilege of Comfort   126

   Conversation Skills   129

   Conversation: Where the Big Ideas Come Together   136

   At Your Desk or in the Halls   139

Epilogue   **141**

References   **143**

Index   **151**

About the Authors   **159**

Preface

During one of my principal walkthroughs, I visited a 7th-grade English language arts classroom where the students were making a list of novels they wanted to read during the annual book challenge. As I circulated throughout the room, I glanced at the book titles on each student's list, taking note of their varied interests in subjects and genres. Jeremy had books that represented his interest in sports, passion for camping, and love of everything gross. One title caught my eye, and I leaned down to offer my thoughts: "Jeremy, this is a great list of novels, but you have a mistake in one of the titles. It's called *To Kill a Mockingbird*, not *How to Kill a Mockingbird*." Jeremy looked up and smiled, and, without saying a word, he politely drew a thick line through the incorrect title, removing it from his list altogether.

This book, much like Harper Lee's renowned work, isn't a manual for the "how-to." Rather than a roadmap of sequential instructions, our purpose lies in articulating the essential conditions required to harness the power of improvement science in service of equity. Rooted in a combined expertise in equity and improvement science, we hold that these realms are not mutually exclusive, but inherently interconnected. Equity absent the tenets of ongoing enhancement lacks direction, while improvement science devoid of a deliberate focus on marginalized voices turns soulless. The confluence of these disciplines hinges on a deep comprehension of the mechanics of transformation, both at an institutional and personal level, though discussions involving equity and change are often intricate and nuanced.

ORIGINS UNVEILED: THE BOOK

This book is grounded in stories. Embedded within are vignettes that bridge the gap between theoretical constructs and lived realities, offering context to the concepts we elaborate. As our shared journey through these pages commences, it seems fitting to unveil the inception behind the book—the inception of our collaborative endeavor. And like any origin tale, there are facts, and there's the essence that seeps in and infuses the narrative, much like honey from a comb.

The idea for this book came about when we were preparing to present at the Carnegie Summit, an annual event sponsored by the Carnegie Foundation for the Advancement of Teaching, which brings "improvers" to California for a few days every spring to share what they are learning about improving. We misunderstood the directions and ended up recording a video to accompany our presentation that was too long to upload to the conference learning management system. But that turned out to be a good thing, because when we listened to the video to make sure that it aligned with what we were going to say in our session, we realized that it covered a lot of conceptual ground and probably could be made into a book. And then when our session went really well, we decided we really needed to write that book. We started work on it right away.

One of the goals of our session at the Carnegie Summit was to get participants to think differently about the relationship between improvement and equity and to surface the ways that we should lean into the human side of change. During the session, we used facilitation moves that provided time for self-reflection and also promoted collaboration and the co-construction of new ideas. Yet these strategies weren't conducive to the written form. Thus, Chapters 2 to 8 conclude with an "At Your Desk or in the Halls" section—a call to reflection and collaboration. Here, you're invited to engage with reflection questions, probing your own practices, embracing growth's challenges, and unsettling established institutional norms—a deliberate disequilibrium.

At your metaphorical desk, we invite you to engage in the three Rs that we see as fundamental steps in individual professional growth and development:

- *Reflect.* Reflection is the cornerstone of growth. It involves taking time to thoughtfully consider your experiences, actions, and outcomes. This self-examination allows you to gain insight into what worked well and what could be improved. Reflecting helps you recognize patterns, strengths, and areas for growth, laying the foundation for intentional progress.
- *Revise.* Building on reflection, revision is the active process of making changes based on your insights. It's about adjusting your approaches, strategies, and methods in response to what you've learned through reflection. This willingness to adapt and refine is key to continuous improvement.
- *Rethink.* Rethinking goes beyond simple adjustments. It involves questioning assumptions and considering alternative perspectives. This step encourages you to explore new ideas, challenge conventional wisdom, and be open to innovative approaches. Rethinking expands your horizons and fosters a growth mindset.

These three Rs guide your individual professional growth by prompting you to engage with your experiences, be adaptable, and embrace the potential for transformation.

In the metaphorical halls, we encourage you to connect with others and engage in the three Rs of collaborative professional growth that highlight the dynamic nature of learning and development:

- *Resonate.* When processing with others, ideas and perspectives resonate. This involves finding common ground and shared understanding. It's about connecting with viewpoints that align with your values and goals, ultimately deepening your own insights.
- *Refine.* Through collaboration, your thoughts and concepts undergo refinement. The diverse inputs from others help polish your ideas, making them more robust and well-rounded. This iterative process hones your thinking and enhances your overall approach.
- *Reimagine.* Collaborative processing sparks the capacity to reimagine possibilities. Exchanging insights with others often leads to creative solutions and fresh perspectives that might not have emerged individually. This openness to new ideas drives innovation and growth.

These Rs highlight how collaboration fosters a rich environment for professional growth, encouraging you to engage with different perspectives, challenge your assumptions, and collectively create meaningful progress.

In embarking on this book, it is paramount to clarify that our intent is not to engage in debate about the existence of systemic oppression. We firmly stipulate that the adversity endured by marginalized groups and the unequal educational outcomes of students cannot be attributed to any inherent deficiencies in ability or character. Nor does it stem solely from the actions of individuals harboring ill intentions, seeking to advance themselves by subjugating others. In truth, our exploration reveals that the manifold experiences and outcomes described earlier find their roots in the interwoven frameworks of oppression deeply entrenched in White supremacy.

It is essential to emphasize that this book does not endeavor to advocate for a hierarchy of oppression. Engaging in a contest to determine which marginalized group faces graver injustices proves counterproductive, fostering division rather than the sense of inclusion and unity that we strive for. Our observations have underscored how this line of thought inadvertently sets marginalized communities against one another, detracting from the overarching goal of nurturing solidarity.

While our comprehension of equity encompasses the diverse narratives of historically marginalized and ostracized individuals, we unapologetically focus many of our discussions on the intricate tapestry of race and racism—specifically anti-Black racism. This is not a narrow viewpoint, but rather a deliberate choice to address the enduring impact of racism, which transcends the actions of individual racists. The roots of systemic racism in the United States extend back half a millennium, conceived as a deliberate construct to dehumanize Black individuals, all while cementing the dominance of White individuals. Although the contours of systemic racism have extended their reach to affect various racial and ethnic groups, it is crucial to acknowledge that anti-Black racism continues to cast its shadow over society. In doing so, we can better appreciate the nuanced threads that form the fabric of inequity, allowing us to navigate toward a future woven with understanding, empathy, and justice.

ORIGINS UNVEILED: THE AUTHORS

For most of the rest of the book, we use the pronoun "we" to designate us as a writing team, as a partnership, and as if we are a single unit; to make the narrative flow more smoothly, we use "we" even if what we're writing about only applies to one of us. But because story is important, here we talk about our individual experiences and how we came to this point in our lives.

At first glance, we may seem like an unlikely pair, or even an odd couple. While Isobel, a White woman, was born in Scotland and came to the United States as an adult, Rydell, a Black man, is a New Jersey native who spent the better part of his adult life in North Carolina. And, as you would expect, the differences in our lived experiences extend far beyond whether we call it a lift or an elevator, a boot or a trunk, or a rubbish bin or trash can.

Though born in Scotland, Isobel lived mostly in England, where having a Scottish accent was a low-status marker at a time when it was still considered acceptable to make fun of people for their accents and stereotypes were aired for amusement. Scots were considered mean in the sense of being overly frugal, and the Irish were considered stupid. When she moved to America, she was amazed to realize that her working-class Scottish accent was reborn as a desirable, cosmopolitan European accent. So she has moved through the world as a low-social-status person and a high-social-status person, and high is better.

Raised by southern parents who saw the Northeast as the land of opportunity, Rydell grew up believing that education was the great equalizer. It wasn't long, however, before he began to recognize the lack of opportunities available to kids of color. As he matured, Rydell learned that, despite the perceived proximity to Whiteness gained from being educated at the "right" schools, living in the "right" neighborhood, and using the "right" speech patterns, his racial identity would always play a significant role in how he was received by others regardless of where he lived. So, in an effort to fit in, he has moved through the world as an inauthentic person hustling for acceptance and as an authentic person willing to paint outside the lines, and authenticity is better.

Collectively, we have lived on three continents, three countries, and seven states. And despite the differences in where we've lived and how we've lived, there is a great deal of overlap in our professional experiences. Most of our time as school-based educators has been spent in schools with high numbers of students of color, students from poverty, and students whose first language was not English. As we reflect, we realize now how easily we accepted the low expectations for our students early in our careers; the low achievement and high dropout rates were normalized in a way that it took us a long time to recognize, and while we can explain that in terms of socialization and psychological distance, it still feels like a sustained failure that we are still accounting for. During that time, site-based decision-making swept through American education, and schools and districts began to write improvement plans with multiple goals and long lists of action items that rarely amounted to anything; the schools most in need of improvement were the ones that had the least capacity to improve themselves.

After teaching high school geography in England and Texas, Isobel transitioned to administration. Isobel got a master's degree in special education and educational leadership, and it was work she did as an administrator in charge of special education that really made her rethink how we base what students are capable of on some arbitrary criteria. She saw that students in America are diagnosed with disabilities in numbers that are completely unthinkable in other countries. At one point, she got feedback about her performance as a leader that put her on a path to learning about psychological growth and development, and she got a PhD in human and organizational systems and became a certified coach. It was also during that time that she read W. Edwards Deming and realized that what he was advocating for in books like *Out of the Crisis* (1982) was the complete opposite of what the proponents of site-based decision-making had led her to believe, so she has been working to change the way that educational leaders think about writing improvement plans for a while now.

After teaching music in New Jersey and North Carolina, Rydell left the glitz and glamour of education to pursue a master's in divinity. It was there that Rydell discovered Black theologians and philosophers like James Cone and Cornel West, liberation theologians like Gustavo Gutiérrez and Leonardo Boff, and womanist theologians like Kelly Brown Douglas and Emilie Townes. These scholars shaped Rydell's understanding of justice and laid the foundation for his belief that God is on the side of the oppressed. After returning to the classroom for a short stint, Rydell decided that he could make a bigger impact as an administrator. He got a master's degree and EdD in educational leadership and worked to operationalize his commitment to social justice as a principal, chief of curriculum and instruction, and superintendent.

Our paths crossed at Partners for Educational Leadership (PEL), a non-profit organization with a mission to improve teaching and learning via improving leadership and coaching, to reduce achievement gaps, and to promote equity in schools. At PEL, our work has been both in equity and improvement science, and as we work to support schools and districts in their improvement efforts, we have learned to focus on the human side of change. Change is a fascinating and complex journey that touches on the essence of what it means to be human. This book is an exploration of the intricate relationship between educational reform, equity, and the human dimensions of change. We hope to shed light on how fostering an equitable, inclusive, and supportive environment for all students is not just a desirable outcome but an essential component of any effective and lasting school improvement efforts.

Acknowledgments

We wish to express our deep appreciation for the friends and colleagues who have shared so much insight so generously on equity and improvement science: David Eddy-Spicer, Brandi Hinnant-Crawford, Kerry Lord, Andrew Volkert, and Tinkhani White. We are grateful to those who gave us feedback on the proposal and early drafts: Amelia Donahey, Amity Goss, Khary Fletcher, Thomas Nobili, and Michael Rafferty. And we are grateful to those who have been so encouraging about this project: Richard Lemons, Ann O'Doherty, Paul Jones, Natalie Simpson, Stephen Higgins, and countless other dedicated educators with whom we work.

We are also indebted to the hundreds of teachers, leaders, coaches, and equity advocates in a multitude of roles who have been with us on this journey, although they may not have known it. We thank them for their work in service of meeting the needs of all students, but especially the marginalized students for whom the educational system at any scale was not designed. We wish the students in schools that are not always kind to them the support, challenge, inspiration, and grace that they so deserve. May their education be worthy of them.

Finally, to our incredible families—your unwavering support and boundless love have been our guiding light throughout this journey. Your belief in us, even during the busiest of times, has been the wind beneath our wings. Thank you for understanding our commitment to education, equity, and the pursuit of a better world. Your encouragement fuels our determination to create positive change, and we are grateful.

CHAPTER 1

Iterative Justice

Before we embark on this exploration of the human factors that impact improvement efforts in the service of equity, let us consider the core premise that underpins our approach. Equity, as a vision, is just a dream without the knowledge, skills, and dispositions to actualize it. Similarly, improvement science, with its focus on data and systematic change, is amoral without a central focus on equity. When the two domains are intertwined, improvement science and equity-focused leadership reinforce and strengthen each other. We hope that educators of all backgrounds will view improvement science as a powerful approach to working toward equity and to see themselves as both improvement scientists and equity advocates.

At the heart of this book lies the concept of liberatory improvement science: when educators embrace improvement science in service of the intentional dismantling of oppressive systems while centering the voices, perspectives, and agency of historically marginalized individuals. Liberatory improvement science goes beyond conventional notions of improvement, recognizing that achieving measurable goals alone is insufficient in the quest for equity. It demands a critical examination of power dynamics, an unwavering commitment to dismantling systemic barriers, and a deep understanding of the lived experiences of those most affected by inequities.

Through this exploration, we invite readers to envision a new narrative in education—one where liberation, equity, and improvement converge. We aim to empower educators to embrace their roles as liberatory improvement scientists, arming them with the knowledge, skills, and dispositions needed to effect systemic change. By grounding our work in the realities of marginalized students and communities, we hope to inspire and equip educators to engage in transformative practices that address the root causes of inequity and work toward a more just and inclusive educational system.

WHY READ THIS BOOK?

In today's educational landscape, the pursuit of equity is a central focus for educational leaders. Which is as it should be: The educational outcomes of marginalized students lag persistently and predictably behind those of their more privileged peers. Frequently, the strategy for improving those outcomes, at least initially, is to "do equity." In other words, educators in schools and districts look at their disaggregated data, set goals, and engage in professional development that includes raising awareness about identity, socialization, implicit bias, stereotypes, and low expectations that, presumably, lead to higher expectations, more challenging instruction, and greater achievement. In the best-case scenario, that actually happens. In the worst-case scenario, student outcomes do not change following data analysis, goal-setting, and professional development (PD) on equity, and so educators conclude that they "did equity" but "it didn't make a difference" and they move on to something else.

We are not suggesting that taking those initial steps is the wrong thing to do, simply that they are among the many steps in what ought to be, but frequently is not, an intentional and thoughtful continuous improvement process. This process should entail the development of a vision for what true equity might look like (one that really does include "all students"), understanding the system that causes inequities in the first place, developing a theory for what to do differently, deciding what to try out, and studying what happens to be increasingly effective. We show these steps in an improvement process map (see Figure 1.1), which we will refer to in other parts of this book.

This map is our way of representing a particular kind of continuous improvement—improvement science—which has come to education via health care (Bryk et al., 2015) but which has its roots in the work of W. Edwards Deming (1982) and his work with Japanese and later American manufacturers after World War II. We, like most educators, were taught in our leadership preparation programs that continuous improvement is a good thing and that we should be engaged in continuous improvement through the creation and implementation of school improvement plans and district strategic plans, benchmarks, and review of data. We had the concept of plan-do-study-act (PDSA) cycles drilled into us. But we were not taught anything practical enough to be useful, and so we tended to think that if our plans were not "living documents" then somehow that was our failure (Stevenson, 2019). We had read Deming and knew that the hard accountability that is frequently attached to plans is something he specifically railed against; we also knew that these plans were very far from alive and mostly lay in suspended animation at the bottom of the office bookshelf. But it wasn't until getting our hands on more technical resources, such as *The Improvement Guide* (Langley et al., 2009) and *Toyota Kata* (Rother, 2009) that we had access to ways of thinking about continuous improvement that were both logical and actionable.

But we have also learned that issues of equity provoke responses in educators that make those issues uniquely difficult to talk about. Students, families, and educators of color have not always been treated with the same respect for their abilities, culture, and point of view as their White peers. People of color have often experienced being ignored, dismissed, or

Figure 1.1. The Improvement Process Map

Improvement Process Map Mark 2

Vision
- *What are we trying to improve, and for whom?*
- *How will we know if the changes we make are an improvement?*

Understand the current system
- What are our current results?
- What are our hypotheses about how the design of our system produces current results?
- Where are the bright spots? What do we know about the places where results are better than others?
- What else could explain our results? Who might have a different or deeper view?
- How can we better understand how the system works?

Focus collective efforts
- Given what we know about our system, where are the "leverage points" where we have the will, ideas & capacity to conduct improvement work?
- What key measures would provide useful, timely feedback about the progress of our improvement work?
- What is our initial theory about what kinds of changes may lead to improvement? How could we represent that visually?

Generate ideas for change
- Building from our theory of improvement, what changes could we try? Do our change ideas align with the "leverage points" in our system?
- Have the people who will be implementing changes been included in generating change ideas? Who else might have ideas?
- Which change ideas would have the biggest impact for our most marginalized students?
- Which change ideas could yield "quick wins," i.e. high impact/relatively low effort to implement?

Cycles of learning in practice
- Having specified a change idea, how might we test out the change at a small scale, quickly & cheaply? ("What can we learn about the change by next Tuesday?")
- What data could help us quickly learn more about process, i.e. how the change works & how we could make it work better?
- What data could help us quickly learn about results, i.e. whether the change is an improvement, for whom & under what conditions?
- What routines (team meetings, data collection, documentation, etc.) will we enact to create iterative, disciplined cycles of testing & improving our change?
- What measures could we monitor over time to understand variation in process & results? How will we look for the bright spots?
- When & how will we plan to periodically consolidate learning from our cycles? How might we update our theory of improvement based on what we are learning?

Sustain & spread

UNDER CONSTRUCTION

Partners for Educational Leadership

contradicted when they bring up concerns about the way that they, their children, or their colleagues are being treated. White educators are almost always well-intentioned, do not espouse any racist beliefs, and find any implication otherwise confusing and upsetting. "Racist" is among the worst epithets that can be applied to a White person, so it is not surprising that the slightest connotation evokes a defensive reaction. Put all these conditions together, and it is not surprising that the safest course of action seems to be to leave the issue well alone. But this is a mistake.

We are educators with a deep commitment to equity who, therefore, want others like us to have the power and the tools to make schools more equitable places. We believe that many of those tools can be taken from the field of improvement science. But we also know that seeking to apply those tools in an equity-neutral way is unlikely to be helpful, for a couple of reasons. First, without an explicit focus on equity, meaning that equity is the goal, then it is easy to work on changes that bring about positive change for some students, or even all students, without having a positive impact on the most marginalized students. And second, an equity goal that is pursued without attention to the voices of individuals who have been marginalized does not feel like equity to those individuals; it feels like a repeat of one of their enduring experiences of life in general, which is to say, being told what's good for them. A couple of examples might be useful here.

Example One. In the early days of No Child Left Behind,[1] the way in which the performance bands were structured meant that schools had an incentive to focus their attention on "bubble kids," meaning those students who scored just below the cutoff for proficiency. Moving enough of those students into the proficiency category might change the performance category of the school itself, which meant that the school might no longer be considered low performing and was therefore no longer subject to the potential sanctions that were part of the law. Schools (like the ones where we worked) were advised by central office staff to focus their school improvement plans on "bubble kids" because they were "low-hanging fruit" in the effort to move up in the performance rankings. We, interestingly, did not argue. As a result, many students who scored just below proficiency on standardized tests received additional attention, which may have taken the form of tutoring, or an extra literacy class, case management by a school counselor, or rewards to perform better on the test. It was possible, therefore,

---

[1] This was the name of the federal Elementary and Secondary Schools Education Act during the first decade of this century; as part of George W. Bush's claim to be a major player in the improvement of educational outcomes for America's children, schools were rated according to their performance on their state's performance accountability metrics, as measured by student achievement, and were subjected to a range of sanctions if their performance did not meet the established benchmark.

that a school could improve its performance without addressing the needs of the lowest-performing students in the school. This is an example of how an equity-neutral policy can bring about improvement without improving equity. Attending a school that had improved its performance rating did not necessarily mean an improvement in the opportunity, experience, or performance of many of the students who most needed such improvements. Which is, of course, sadly ironic given that the name of the law was No Child Left Behind.

Example Two. Equity goals without the participation of those most affected by them may also lead to unfortunate circumstances. Educators making decisions about how to pursue those goals often assume that they know how to achieve them, but maybe they don't. A common equity-related goal is for schools to increase the number of students of color in Advanced Placement (AP) classes, presumably because this is an indicator that the school's high academic expectations apply to all students, not just the White students. If school administrators assume that students of color are not enrolling in AP classes because they are not aware of them, or that they don't know they are eligible for them, or that they are not aware of the potential benefits of taking AP, then they will launch an information campaign that apprises students and their families of these things. But in one school that had a goal of increasing enrollment of students of color in AP courses, the principal suggested that before they launched such a campaign, the assistant principals and counselors talk to the students of color themselves.

So they conducted student focus groups, and they discovered that the students were already aware of the information that the assistant principals and counselors had assumed that they lacked. And they were choosing to not enroll in AP courses for all sorts of reasons, including they were worried about their grades in those courses because they wanted to maintain eligibility for sports, they were concerned that they wouldn't feel welcome in courses that often had no students of color enrolled in them, and they were worried about the workload when they had other obligations and interests outside of school and didn't believe that the teachers would cut them much slack. A plan for change that failed to involve the people that the change hoped to help would have been a waste of time and energy and would have reinforced the belief held by many people of color that those in charge don't believe that people of color know what's good for them and need help figuring that out.

The purpose of this book, in the briefest of terms, is to elucidate the equity-specific knowledge, skills, and dispositions that are required for educators to use improvement science to make schools more equitable places. We begin with the premise that a focus on equity is feeble without knowledge, skills, and dispositions to make good on that vision and that improvement science is amoral without a focus on equity. In this book, we hope to engage equity advocates who might benefit from employing techniques of improvement science and improvers who want to be more explicitly focused on equity and give them ways of thinking about the overlap between their experiences and interests, so that they will have the language and tools to inform their practice moving forward. We want educators of all backgrounds to view improvement science as an approach to working toward equity and to see themselves as *both* improvement scientists and equity advocates.

We believe that if you are not working toward equity, you're not doing the right work. And if your work on equity does not go beyond conscious raising to improve the system that produces inequity, your efforts will not be as productive as they might be. We take inspiration from the work of Brandi Hinnant-Crawford (2020), who writes: "*But the fight for justice and equality is iterative and continuous. But iterative does not mean slow or stalling; it means constantly reviewing the strategy to get to the goal faster* (p. 211)." And so, what we are attempting to do in this book is to describe and explain the conditions that need to be created to harness improvement science in pursuit of equity, so that your students are more successful and you reach your goals faster. We write, therefore, less about the process of improvement science itself (you should read Brandi's book for that) and more about the human side of change—the factors that make it more or less likely that an inclusive vision will be created, that the system will be understood from the perspective of *all* stakeholders, and that improvement will be enacted in a way that will most likely lead to success for all.

Throughout this book we have tried to challenge some of the conventional wisdom in the arena of school reform that we think is unhelpful—that change is scary, that accountability is a high-leverage tool for advancing equity, that improvement science is interested only in quantitative data, to name a few. But we agree with the common assertion that change is messy—and in fact, we think it's messier than is commonly realized. It is messy because systems don't always operate the way you expect them to; because people are complicated and many of the common assumptions about them are wrong; because checklists, tools, and protocols are useful but not as powerful as is frequently thought; and because inequity benefits so many. Our hope is that a more critical examination of the human factors that influence education reform will make educators more aware, more intentional, and more resilient when change does not come easy and improvement is hard to discern.

MENTAL MODELS AND INSTITUTIONAL LOGICS

Improvement science is, for us, a path for moving beyond those first steps of consciousness raising around equity toward meaningful change in systems and practices that actually make a difference for marginalized students. Bringing equity and improvement science together, however, is hindered by their ostensible competing institutional logics—the broad principles that guide a collective endeavor or organization and represent what is widely valued in that organization, reinforced and rewarded, and believed to lead to success. Educators engaged in the collective endeavor of improvement science often embrace a set of principles laid out in Bryk et al. (2015):

1. Make the work problem-specific and user-centered;
2. Focus on variation in performance;
3. See the system that produces current outcomes;
4. We cannot improve at scale what we cannot measure;
5. Use disciplined inquiry to drive improvement;
6. Accelerate learning through networked communities.

There is nothing here that conflicts with equity as an overarching goal or mission. But educators who draw on a different institutional logic often have a mental model of improvement science as a clinical and technical process, with a focus on measurable outcomes and data-driven decision-making that is incompatible with a commitment to equity, whose institutional logics are focused on people, history, righteousness, and justice. Improvement science as a field has not always been seen as embracing equity as a central goal of the work of improvement. As a result, educators whose primary focus is improving equity have been suspicious and sometimes dismissive of improvement science (Safir & Dugan, 2021). As Bush-Mecenas (2022) explains, "With its roots in Taylorism and the Total Quality Control movement in industry, [continuous improvement] is typically a highly routinized, scientific process to promote incremental changes that improve efficiency, productivity, and profitability. While the goals of efficiency and productivity are not necessarily at odds with promoting equity, the underlying assumptions and means typically associated with these goals can diverge substantially" (p. 461).

Even those who realize that the strengths of improvement science can be used for good do not necessarily embrace it as a primary tool for engineering equity; "you can't PDSA your way to total system transformation" has become something of a mantra. We do not agree that improvement science is impotent when it comes to system transformation. We do concede that it hasn't happened much. Nonetheless, while we are waiting for the revolution, it couldn't hurt to leverage improvement science to improve equity in our schools. And, increasingly, there are stories available to us of how school districts have learned to do this (see, for example, Bryk et al., 2023). But also, while system transformation is an inspiring vision, it mostly lies outside the power of the majority of educators, but these same educators can reasonably work together to improve the lives of students in ways that may not be revolutionary but are nevertheless substantial and should not be underestimated or undervalued.

IMPROVING TOGETHER

We know that there are equity advocates in education who would like to harness the methods of improvement science but find the technical aspects daunting. Likewise, we know that there are many educators who have expertise and experience in improvement science who would like to be more centered on equity work but find that that community, too, is not always easy to enter. We want educators with a background in equity to have experience with tools and ideas that demonstrate the utility of improvement science to further their aims. Likewise, we want educators with experience and expertise in improvement science to recognize that many of the fundamental principles of improvement science absolutely map to the principles of equity. So in this chapter we attempt to explain why we think that equity and improvement science are such a good match for each other.

If we've learned nothing else in the last 20 years, it is that equity issues in education are complex and multifaceted, involving multiple stakeholders with different perspectives, interests, and power dynamics. To achieve meaningful improvements in outcomes for all students, including those from marginalized and disadvantaged backgrounds, it is essential to take a nuanced, culturally responsive, and socially just approach to managing change. Addressing equity issues in education requires a deep understanding of the underlying systemic and structural factors that contribute to disparities in outcomes. Traditional approaches to improvement science may not be sufficient on their own to address these complex issues if they focus more on addressing discrete problems and improving specific processes and outcomes.

While most "equity work" encourages educators to look at student outcome data to identify the problems that should be addressed, it seldom includes mining the experiences of stakeholders on the margins to identify change ideas. Improvement science relies heavily on the use of evidence-based practices. Unfortunately, the evidence base in education may not always reflect the needs and experiences of all students, particularly those from historically marginalized and underserved communities. Therefore, there may be a need for a more nuanced and culturally responsive approach to using evidence-based practices that takes into account the specific needs of different student populations and, more importantly, centers marginalized stakeholders—students, staff, and families—in the development and curation of potential change ideas. Further, approaches that rely heavily on quantitative data-driven decision-making can perpetuate existing inequities if the data are not representative of all students or if the data reinforce the deficit thinking about marginalized students—especially students of color.

Assuming that improvement science is only about the collection of quantitative data in order to design clinical interventions fails to capture the complexity and nuance of the improvement process. In reality, improvement science is a collaborative and iterative approach that requires ongoing sense-making and adaptation along the way. This approach is especially important when the improvement focus is on equity because improvement efforts often involve multiple stakeholders with diverse perspectives and priorities.

WHAT DO WE MEAN BY EQUITY, AND WHY DO WE WANT IT?

We think of equity in terms of access, opportunity, experience, and outcomes for students. Equity in education is achieved when student outcomes are not predicted by gender, race, ethnicity, class, sexual orientation, language, or ability and when all students reach a level of efficacy and competence that supports a rewarding and productive life. This requires the amelioration of the biases and processes in the system that contribute to disproportionate access, opportunity, learning, and achievement by marginalized students.

In America, perceptions and biases about race, class, ability, and gender have deep roots bound into our national history, culture, systems, and structures. By default, these perceptions and biases are replicated in schools.

- Inequities based on racism and classism are baked into our educational system and must be dismantled at a personal, institutional, and systemic level—it is the system that causes the inequities, not the student.
- Educational inequities are caused by racism, prejudice, and bias that disadvantage marginalized groups.
- Working on institutional racism without working on personal and interpersonal transformation allows inequities to persist and subverts systemic transformation.
- Ensuring equity in schools requires a deep commitment to and accountability for high-quality teaching and learning.

Despite all the attention being paid to equity at the moment in American education, there are still pervasive misunderstandings about the benefits of greater equity.

There are some persistent assumptions among many districts at the beginning of their equity journey. We discuss some of them here:

1. *Equity is only an issue when the district has a significant number of students of color.* This assumes that White students are somehow not implicated in social justice unless they are in proximity to students of color

and that race and racism have salience only to people of color. Associating equity with race also precludes thinking about all the other ways that students can be discriminated against or marginalized: their gender and gender identity, ability and disability, religion, sexual orientation, nationality and migrant status, and housing and economic status. Equity is not an issue only when all students are high achieving, are intellectually challenged, have access to the academic and emotional supports they need, feel physically and psychologically safe, and are treated with what they consider to be dignity and respect.

2. *The locus of the problem of low achievement, high dropout rates, or behavioral concerns rests with the performance of individuals rather than baked into how the system operates.* Despite what educational leaders are taught in their university preparation programs about systems thinking, they sometimes fall back on their assumptions that the root of the problem is the lack of commitment, motivation, and resources of students and their families, on the one hand, and the low expectations of teachers for marginalized students, on the other. This has the effect of placing influence over the concerns furthest away from the educators' circle of control, and it is hard to solve a problem when you don't have power to affect the factors that cause it. As James Baldwin (1962) said, "Not everything that is faced can be changed; but nothing can be changed until it is faced" (p. 38).

3. *Raising teachers' awareness of race, stereotypes, and implicit bias will inevitably lead to better outcomes for marginalized students.* But as discussed earlier in this chapter, the work on equity in education is often around raising awareness and building educators' personal capacity. And indeed, we all have biases, which translates generally into lower expectations and discriminatory practices against students of color especially, but not exclusively, by White educators. In particular, Black students are more likely to be disciplined, they're more likely to be referred for special education, and their outcomes are likely to be lower. But once these discrepancies are recognized, there's still the question of redress: What do we actually do to improve access, experience, and outcomes for marginalized students? Awareness is not enough; there has to be a mechanism for making sure that low expectations aren't played out in real life. This is why we believe that equity and improvement science belong together.

4. *Equity is a separate body of work from the main district strategy for improvement.* We have been in too many situations when it became clear that the superintendent saw equity as pertaining to a subset of students in the district—most often students of color, but perhaps also

students with identified disabilities—and not as central to the district vision. This, on the face of it, makes no sense, as the majority of school districts have a vision or mission statement that refers to "all students"; nevertheless, for many leaders, they don't have to concern themselves with equity unless and until they are faced with issues involving students of color or they are forced to because of an incident, such as a racial epithet used at a football game or a swastika drawn on the locker of a Jewish student. But reaching a vision that includes all students does in fact entail confronting the variations that exist within classrooms, schools, and districts and figuring out how to eliminate them (Irby, 2022).

5. *Equity is getting people more of what's good for them.* Many discussions of equity are fundamentally paternalistic. Teachers, leaders, and others in power hold the assumption that either they are the experts in the field and therefore know what students and families need to do in order to be successful or they are the people in power and therefore get to decide what success looks like, and possibly both. A fundamental premise in both equity and improvement science is that educators should always be asking two questions: Who is impacted? And who is involved? Those questions should lead not only to the involvement of marginalized students and their families and communities in solutions for problems but also to their involvement in defining those problems in the first place. Who gets to decide how to frame an issue as a problem is just as much a function of how power is wielded as how to generate and implement a solution.

6. *Equity is a zero-sum game; gains for some necessitate losses for others.* We worked with a district on their desire to become an antiracist organization; at the beginning of one meeting, the superintendent talked about equity as being the right thing to do, but that he understood that if there was greater equity in education, then his own children would have to work harder to get ahead and that they would necessarily lose some of their privilege. We recognize that this is a common idea, but it bears some unpacking. The zero-sum game mentality assumes two things: that the amount of whatever is in question (money, for example) is forever fixed, and therefore, in order for one person to have more, others will have to have less. However, this is not accurate. Economies expand and contract, and having a better-qualified workforce is one of the factors that contribute to economic growth. It used to be the case that women were prohibited from holding paying jobs outside the home because it was assumed that they were automatically taking a job from a man who needed the money to support their family. But now women make up almost half of the paid labor force in the United States, and removing them from those jobs would be a catastrophe for the economy. Likewise, many manifestations of inequity are a drag on the economy. For example, the

unbelievably high number of incarcerated Black men is a human rights issue, but also an economic issue, because incarceration is expensive, and incarceration removes people from the workforce. At the same time, if that superintendent is thinking about privilege as unearned and unfair advantage, then improved equity would indeed have the effect of removing privilege from his children, and that's a good thing. It is also the case that people with privilege would rather keep that privilege, even if it means being worse off in economic terms, than have more in absolute terms but lose status relative to others, especially when those others are of a "lower" race and class (McGhee, 2022).

Equity, then, is a moral imperative; it is simply right and fair that every student has what they need to be successful. But equity is also economically desirable; we feel the need to point this out because if there are educators who think that they are working against their own, or their children's, self-interest in promoting equity, it is hard to see how they can be expected to be enthusiastic allies. If equity in schools means that all students graduate healthier, happier, and better qualified to be successful in the vocation of their choosing, we will all be better off.

WHY IMPROVEMENT SCIENCE AND EQUITY HAVE MORE IN COMMON THAN YOU MIGHT THINK

As Bush-Mecenas points out, at first glance, improvement science and equity appear to be mutually repellent institutional logics. But we argue that, in fact, they share many assumptions; here, we identify those commonalities and explain why they are significant.

Systems Thinking. "Every system is perfectly designed to get the result it gets." This is an oft-cited maxim attributed to the Institute of Healthcare Improvement's Paul Batalden. The point is, at one level, that we should think about outcomes in terms of the interactions between and among components of our system. And at another level, the point is that we should stop blaming people for outcomes that are not completely under their control; if we want different results, we have to change the system that creates them (Deming, 1982). Most educators are familiar with these ideas; they are taught in leadership preparation classes, they are featured in many books popular with educators, and they appear frequently in memes and gifs on the Internet. And yet, many policies aimed at improving outcomes for students continue to rest on the assumption that, indeed, if high expectations for outcomes are set, and if pressure is exerted through exposure and consequences, then outcomes will improve.

Our current methods of accountability appear to rely on two tools: a spotlight and a hammer. But if it is the case that the results we see are created by an existing system, then the system itself has to change. Changing a system, whether that system is a car engine, an organization, or a human body, requires tools. So, if we want different results, the questions we need to ask are: What kind of system can produce those results? And what kind of tools do we need to make that system? Our contention is that a spotlight and a hammer probably aren't all that is required. In fact, not only do we need different tools—we probably need a whole other toolkit.

Equity and improvement science both espouse the following principle: "Be hard on systems, soft on people." The system is perfectly designed to produce the results it gets; therefore, there is little point in blaming the educators, the students, or the families for outcomes that are created by the system in which they are embedded. Understanding the system and why it produces the outcomes it produces is thus an essential part of both improvement science and equity.

Experience. People's experience is hugely important to them. It connects to their sense of belonging, their perceived self-efficacy, their mental models about how the world operates, and their mindsets about themselves: whether they can handle stressful situations, whether they are an athlete, whether they can go to college, whether they can rebound from setbacks. The experiences of the people within the system are not incidental to system outcomes. As we described in Example Two earlier about enrollment in AP classes, what students said about why they did or did not enroll in those classes gave the educators at the school plenty of information about how the system worked, that they could then use to think about where in the system a change might lead to an improvement. In improvement science, this is often referred to as UX, which stands for "user experience," a term drawn from design thinking (Kolko, 2014). That term seems a little cold to those of us who have worked with students and families who have been discounted by the system, but one of the most important tools in learning about the user experience is the empathy interview, and that has been part of equity-focused change for some time (Safir, 2017).

Bias. For equity advocates, bias is usually associated with racial bias, which at the individual level is the (often unconscious) preconceptions about people from different racial groups and at an institutional or societal level is the factors that cause disparate outcomes for people of color. Racial bias is well-documented and includes discrimination against job candidates with names associated with being Black, lower house appraisals for homes belonging to Black families, and care for Black women about to give birth that is less sensitive to potential problems for mother and child and can be life-threatening

(Eberhardt, 2019). All of these can be true, and yet it is also true that the employers, appraisers, and medical professionals implicated in these cases may have no espoused racist beliefs. Perhaps the most common form of bias is deficit thinking: the belief that marginalized students have problems, or are problems, because they (and their families) have traits that interfere with academic performance, such as lack of motivation, lack of commitment to education, lack of background knowledge, and so on. Deficit thinking perpetuates inequity by reinforcing low expectations ("my kids can't do that, they're well below grade level"), pathologizing ("the problem is they don't get any support from home"), and catastrophizing ("those kids will never be able to . . . "). People in the system frequently have more strengths than they are given credit for; eliminating unconscious bias takes conscious effort.

Racial bias is pernicious, but not the only form of bias. Bias can mean prejudice in favor of, or against, one person or group, but it can also mean a predictable and pervasive distortion, such as cognitive bias. To be human is to have cognitive biases; we simply are not as rational as we think we are, and we fall prey to ways of thinking about making decisions that lead to suboptimal outcomes. Some of the best-known cognitive biases are sunk-cost fallacy, wherein we make decisions based on how much time or money we have already expended, rather than what is now in our best interest; recency bias, which means that we tend to overestimate the importance of what has just happened in estimating the probability of future events; and halo effect, when people who have desirable qualities in one sphere are assumed to have them in others, so that attractive people (according to social norms such as tall in height and low in body weight) are assumed to be more competent than those perceived as less attractive.

Leadership brings its own set of biases. Leaders, especially male leaders (Chamorro-Premuzic, 2019), have too much faith in their own judgment, which leads to suboptimal outcomes in talent management, surgery, piloting airplanes, and countless other fields (Edmondson, 2012). These findings ring true for us; it is our experience that leaders assume that they have more knowledge and understanding of challenges than they really do and tend to believe that they are qualified, entitled, and expected to diagnose, prescribe, and monitor problems and their solutions. Contrary to the belief of many leaders, expertise and power are not synonymous, and hierarchies are, as a result, more dangerous than helpful; as we will see in Chapter 6, rank and power interfere with objectivity and rationality in ways that people in power are frequently blind to.

Pragmatism. Pragmatism is a philosophical approach that emphasizes practicality, usefulness, and the importance of practical consequences in determining the truth or value of ideas. Pragmatism focuses on practical outcomes and problem-solving rather than adhering to fixed ideologies or abstract theories. It places value on experimentation, flexibility, and adaptation in order to achieve desired results. In the context of education, pragmatism trumps ideology by prioritizing the practical application of ideas and strategies to improve educational outcomes. Instead of rigidly adhering to a particular educational ideology or theory, educational leaders who embrace pragmatism focus on what works in practice and adapt their approaches based on evidence and outcomes. They are willing to set aside ideological preconceptions and embrace ideas and methods that are proven to be effective.

Educators who emphasize improvement science and those committed to equity share a pragmatic disposition in their approach to improving outcomes. As pragmatists, improvers have been creative in drawing from the work of scholars and practitioners in other fields, including, for example, work on high-reliability organizations (Weick & Roberts, 1993), design thinking, wicked problems, sense-making (Weick, 1995), and positive deviance. Improvement science is, therefore, more pragmatic than ideological, as improvers are not afraid to draw on other traditions and institutional logics.

Similarly, pragmatic equity advocates prioritize the real-world impact of their work—addressing systemic barriers and disparities in education to ensure that all students have equal opportunities for success. They recognize the need for adaptation and flexibility in their approaches and understand that solutions may vary based on context and that there is no one-size-fits-all approach to achieving equity. Pragmatists embrace experimentation, flexibility, and learning from experience, while equity advocates are attuned to the specific needs of diverse student populations. By being pragmatic, equity advocates can continuously adapt their strategies, making necessary adjustments to effectively address equity issues in their classrooms and schools.

Improvement work is both adaptive and technical. Pragmatic improvers and equity advocates understand that the work of improving outcomes and promoting equity is multifaceted. It requires both adaptive and technical approaches. Adaptive work involves addressing complex, dynamic challenges that require shifts in mindsets, beliefs, and behaviors. Technical work, on the other hand, focuses on applying existing knowledge and strategies to solve specific problems. By recognizing the interplay between adaptive and technical work, a pragmatic approach to improvement helps educators navigate complex issues while also utilizing proven practices to drive improvement and promote equity.

Look outside and inside the system for answers. Pragmatic improvers and equity advocates are not limited to looking for solutions exclusively within the existing system. They are willing to explore ideas and practices from outside the system, recognizing that valuable insights and approaches can be found in diverse contexts, disciplines, or sectors. At the same time, they acknowledge that solutions can also emerge from within the system itself. They are open to tapping into the expertise and experiences of individuals within their educational communities, understanding that local knowledge and insights can be instrumental in driving improvement and achieving equity.

VALUES THAT RUN THROUGH THIS BOOK

As with all humans, who we are and the experiences we've had heavily influence everything we do, including our writing. Since so much of the rationale for writing this book is based on embracing specific values and ways of seeing the world, we want to be explicit early on about what those are and why we think they are important. We come to this work with decades of experience in schools and other organizations, of working toward equity, of continuous improvement, and of supporting the professional and personal growth of individuals. In the last few years, we have come to understand that these bodies of work are connected in important ways, and to do any of them well means being aware of those connections and having the confidence and competence to apply knowledge about all of them to making the world, and specifically schools, a better place for students.

Centering Equity. As Ibram Kendi has pointed out, there is no such thing as equity-neutral; a program, policy, or approach to improvement is either racist or antiracist (Kendi, 2019); to fail to challenge the status quo is to support the status quo, and since the status quo in education, as in all other facets of American life, is inherently inequitable, to support the status quo is to perpetuate inequity. This is challenging when our vision is often just a polished-up version of the status quo; we use the analogy of laundry detergent when it is marketed as "new and improved" when in reality the improvement is not noticeably different from the previous version. At the same time, we do not wish to dismiss small improvements over time; as long as they are indeed focused on equity, they may amount to significant changes over time. The idea of centering equity appears in all the chapters of this book—it is our overarching concern, beginning with the next chapter, "Centering the Experiences of Students."

The Power of Story. Much of the way that humans make sense of the world is through telling, and listening to, stories. We internalize values by listening to the stories that we are told as children, by our families, and in other values-driven organizations, such as our places of worship, the Scouts, and schools. Story, memory, and experience are very closely tied together, and so in order to understand how people's experiences have shaped their attitudes, expectations, motivations, and aspirations, we have to listen to their stories. To that end, we talk about the power of story in several places in this book. First, we wish to point out that the improvement process map (Figure 1.1 at the beginning of this chapter) centers questions. Chapter 2 is about centering student experience in our improvement work and the role of stories and storytelling in collecting and leveraging those stories. Chapter 3 includes a discussion of empathy, grace, and understanding, which are developed through listening to people's stories. And Chapter 8 is mostly about the power of conversation, which is, of course, listening to, and co-construction of, story.

Belief in People. Despite what we have written about people and their very human flaws and biases, we have enormous faith in people: to work together; to have empathy, compassion, and grace; to tackle wicked problems; to grow, change and improve. Our years of working with people in coaching and the ministry have taught us that everyone has a story, everyone is doing the best they can, and everyone wants to do better. Great things can happen when the conditions are right for conversations to turn into agreements and actions. Our faith in people shows up throughout the book. Notably, Chapter 3 asks that educators learn skills and stances that will enable them to tap into the experience and wisdom of others in order to understand a situation from multiple points of view. Chapter 5 is about the human side of change and attempts to reframe people's motivation to change away from fear-based explanations and deficit thinking toward what is known about people's motivation to feel competent and their ability to work enthusiastically and endlessly toward a challenge that matches their perceived self-efficacy. And Chapter 8 is about the power of conversations, in which we discuss why conversations are important and what makes them difficult but what also makes them powerful when your faith in people to do good comes through.

CHAPTER 2

Centering the Experiences of Students

In a recent session with our community of practice of equity directors, we had leaders reflect on how their work directly impacted students in their district. We asked them to consider the experiences of a fictitious 10th-grade student named Drew—a Black, queer, cis-gender male who struggles academically and is currently attending one of the high schools represented by the group (see Figure 2.1). After completing the first task, we asked them to repeat the process with a focus on a fictitious sophomore named Jason—a White, heterosexual, cis-gender male who consistently meets or exceeds academic expectations (see Figure 2.2).

Figure 2.1. Drew's Current Experiences

- It's likely that he hears "F" slur or "N" word on a regular basis, even if it's not directed towards him.
- He probably doesn't encounter texts with queer characters or encounter texts written by persons of color ouside of oppression narrative.
- He has friends and has supportive connections with GSA club members.
- He likely hangs out primarily with other students of color.
- He might not feel safe to be "out" to family, peers, etc.
- He sees/experiences other students of color being disproportionately disciplined.
- He is taught by very few (if any) BIPOC staff members of color.
- He may feel he needs to code switch or silence opinion (anger/frustration), so he is not perceived as "angry black kid."
- He may be viewed as disrespectful when disengaged.
- He is on a lower academic track and his schedule is probably filled with intervention/assigned study hall instead of "flex" privileges like other students.

Figure 2.2. Jason's Current Experiences

- He can say probably whatever he wants with little recourse.
- In general, he feels very comfortable.
- He encounters a lot of texts with characters like him.
- He learns history in a way that validates his identity and makes him feel powerful.
- He knows that LGBTQ+ are in his school and has a good idea of who they are.
- He likely gets selected for awards and recognitions.
- His teachers look like him and share many of his same lived experiences.
- He knows that if he gets in trouble, it's usually a verbal consequence because adults see his mistakes as moments or instances, not a part of who he is being.
- He rarely feels or is made to feel shame.
- In general, he feels respected by others and "protected" by a strong peer group.
- He has autonomy and can pick his classes.
- His counselor validates his aspirations and pushes him to go higher/harder.
- People expect him to have good grades, be on the honor roll and take advantage of leadership opportunities at the school.

We gave the directors time to compare the two descriptions and discuss how their experiences would differ from district to district. Despite the diversity of the districts represented, they believed Drew's and Jason's experiences would be similar regardless of which high school they attended. We then asked the directors to describe what a typical day would look like for Drew and Jason in the future—after creating and sustaining a more equitable and socially just environment (see Figure 2.3 and Figure 2.4).

After presenting their descriptions, the groups were asked to identify three equity goals that they imagined would shift the students' current experiences to "one fine day." They were told that they would present their proposed goals to a panel of stakeholders that included Drew and Jason. What followed was fascinating. Initially, the groups talked about traditional approaches to the work: increasing student access to high-quality instruction, reduction of discipline disparities, and the provision of inclusive curriculum and resources. But they quickly realized the flaw in their thinking; they had a hard time connecting their goals and strategies to the lived experiences of Drew and Jason in a genuine and meaningful way. It wasn't that they were unwilling or unable to consider the experiences

Figure 2.3. Drew's Future Experiences

- He experiences less hate speech and knows it is not tolerated by the ways adults and fellow students respond when they hear it.
- He hears other students speaking out against hate speech.
- He encounters texts that represent a variety of identities—queer authors of color; characters of color outside of oppression narrative—achievement, contribution, culture-affirming, sustaining.
- He has more choice to import identity into his academic experience and those of others—a contibutor of content.
- The GSA club is now flourishing and has varied membership; they're focused on activism.
- He feels safe to be "out"—surrounded by supportive peer allies and/or can exist without fear of being full self.
- He feels like a "good child" who is supported when he makes mistakes or bad choices.
- He feels like staff members know his name and care about him as a person.
- He has a more diverse group of teachers that share his identities.
- He is confident and willing to speak his mind, share his perspectives and experiences.
- He feels comfortable having strong opinions without it being a reflection/fulfillment of his identity as stereotype.
- He is more willing to engage because the content and pedagogy are more relevant.
- He still hangs out with other students of color but has also developed a more diverse peer group.
- He gets the academic support he needs to increase his achievement and it's not at the expense of his personal enrichment or a more complete school experience.

of students; they were struggling to center their experiences. Eventually they came around and shifted their approach by asking different questions. Instead of asking: *How will our restorative approach to discipline, which is focused on addressing the teachers' biases, impact the students?*, they asked: *What does Drew need us to do to reduce the likelihood of him hearing racist and homophobic slurs throughout the day?* This slight change in perspective pushed them to think more iteratively and identify change ideas that they would want to try out. After a few minutes, they asked if Drew could join their group to help develop the plan going forward. Shortly after revisiting their profiles and thinking about what Drew and Jason would say about the differences in their daily experiences, they realized that the variation that needed to be addressed was the students' sense of belonging.

Figure 2.4. Jason's Future Experiences

- He doesn't have to hear hate speech from peers and he is expected to take action and stand up for others if he does.
- He is empowered to recognize and stand up against hate.
- His safety is improved because others around him feel safer.
- He encounters people like him and people who are different from me in my studies because diverse lived experiences are represented in his curriculum and because his classmates are encouraged to share their personal stories.
- He learns from other perspectives and experiences and gains a fuller and more accurate sense of the world.
- He is challenged with diverse opinions and develop skills of mutual respect for others.
- He still gets plenty of awards but he is joined by others who are acknowledged for accomplishments that previously went unnoticed.

During our debrief, we discussed the need for a disciplined approach to improvement that prioritizes a deep dive into understanding the system through the eyes of students. We also explored what it means to be student-centered and how that differs from centering the experiences of students. And as we are centering their experiences, we discussed whose experiences matter most. In this chapter, we begin by exploring many of these same ideas. We then discuss common methods for capturing students' experiences and gauging students' sense of belonging.

STUDENT CENTERED VERSUS CENTERING STUDENTS

As we sat to work on this chapter, we tried to think of any educators we have encountered throughout our careers who would openly reject to taking a student-centered approach to schooling. As expected, we came up empty. Our inability to identify individuals who oppose a student-centered approach is not because there is widespread agreement on the best ways to meet the needs of students. It's because the definition of student-centered learning has become so broad that every instructional or leadership move that is made with students at the forefront is considered student centered. Student-centered learning can have various interpretations and cover a range of instructional methods and academic programs. This makes it challenging to pinpoint its exact meaning without any context, specific instances, or further clarification. Sometimes, the term carries a precise and technical connotation, while in other cases, it becomes obscure jargon that's hard to decipher.

The idea of a student-centered approach in education has been shaped by various educational philosophies, theories, and research findings. In the late 19th and early 20th centuries, educational reformers like John Dewey and Maria Montessori championed hands-on learning and engaging students' interests. Constructivist theories from thinkers like Jean Piaget and Lev Vygotsky emphasized learners actively constructing knowledge through interactions. Humanistic psychologists like Carl Rogers stressed individual autonomy and personal growth, while cognitive psychology highlighted active learning and critical thinking. As research on effective teaching and learning unfolded, educators like Benjamin Bloom emphasized student engagement and higher-order thinking skills. All these influences, combined with the recognition of students' diverse needs, have contributed to the popularity of student-centered approaches in education today. Over time, these influences and research findings, along with the recognition of the diverse needs and interests of students, have contributed to the development and popularization of student-centered approaches in education. Today, student-centered education is seen as a promising approach to meet the needs of individual learners, foster engagement, and prepare students for success in a rapidly changing world.

For the sake of our current discussion, we believe being student centered in education means designing teaching and learning experiences that prioritize the needs, interests, and aspirations of students. It places the student at the center of the educational process and recognizes their active role in their own learning. Rather than focusing solely on delivering information and content, a student-centered approach involves privileging their thinking and responding to that.

When we talk about being student centered in education, we're referring to an approach that places the student at the center of the learning experience. On the other hand, centering the experiences of students goes beyond just considering their needs and interests. It involves recognizing and valuing the lived experiences, identities, and perspectives that students bring to the classroom. It acknowledges that students come from diverse cultural, social, and personal backgrounds, and those experiences shape how they engage with the educational process. Centering their experiences means incorporating their voices, stories, and cultural references into the curriculum and instructional practices, making the learning more relevant and meaningful to them.

In essence, being student-centered focuses on the learning process itself, emphasizing instructional strategies that meet students' needs and promote active learning. On the other hand, centering the experiences of students goes deeper, acknowledging the social and cultural contexts that shape students' identities and integrating those experiences into the learning environment. This recognition helps create a more inclusive and culturally responsive classroom that fosters a sense of belonging among students.

When students feel a sense of belonging, they are more willing to share their thoughts, ask questions, and collaborate with their peers. They feel comfortable expressing themselves, knowing that their perspectives are valued and appreciated. This promotes a positive and inclusive learning atmosphere that enhances student engagement, motivation, and overall academic achievement.

BELONGING AND IDENTITY

In *Belonging*, Geoffrey Cohen (2022) emphasizes the crucial importance of educators focusing on their students' sense of belonging. A strong sense of belonging in the classroom positively impacts academic performance, socioemotional well-being, and overall engagement in learning. Belonging is about relationships and connectedness. We all have experienced the discomfort and awkwardness that comes from feeling like you don't belong. When people share positive stories about belonging, they often talk about their feelings—feeling connected to others, feeling unconditionally seen and heard, and feeling valued for who they are and the contributions they bring to the group. When people share negative stories about belonging or recount experiences in which they felt alienated, they tend to focus on how their identity/identities challenged their ability to feel wholly accepted.

Belonging, therefore, is not just about an individual's physical or social reality; it is about the way they perceive their situation. Our perceptions are largely shaped by our identity—how we see ourselves (individual identity) and how we see ourselves in relationship to others (social identity)—and our identity is shaped by how we perceive the world around us. Cohen highlights the connection between sense of belonging and identity in his discussion of how Black college students interpreted adversity on campus: "Black students tend to interpret their belonging uncertainty as stemming from being a minority on campus" (p. 42). In other words, while a specific challenge may be common among all students, the way in which it is perceived is closely tied to the individual students' identity. Therefore, if we are serious about centering students' experiences, we need to better understand identity and uncover the ways it impacts students' lived experiences in our schools.

In this next section, we delve into identity. Understanding students' lived experiences is a crucial aspect of fostering an inclusive and equitable learning environment. Central to this understanding is the recognition of the pivotal role that identity plays in shaping individuals' perceptions, interactions, and aspirations. Identity development is a complex process that encompasses both individual and social aspects. At the individual level, students' identities are molded by personal experiences, beliefs, values, and unique attributes. Simultaneously, social identities, such as race, ethnicity, gender, sexuality, and socioeconomic status, profoundly influence how individuals navigate the world and interact with others. Marginalized students, in particular, face unique challenges and complexities in their identity development as they grapple with societal norms and biases that may adversely impact their self-esteem and academic achievement. By delving into the intricacies of identity development, educators and institutions can gain profound insights into students' perspectives, enabling them to create supportive and inclusive learning environments that celebrate diversity and promote student success.

Individual Identity. Exploring identity is one of the most significant tasks of adolescence. This feat is not accomplished independently; rather, identity development and/or identity construction is the result of engaging in a communal dance of reflections and negotiations in which an adolescent encounters individual characteristics, family, historical influences, and social and political contexts (Harrison, 2015). Although negotiating one's identity is a lifelong process that extends into adulthood (Cross & Fletcher, 2009; Faulkner & Hecht, 2011; Head, 2002), adolescence signifies the onset of identity development (Erikson, 1968). Psychosocial developmental theorists cite biological changes as the reason students begin identity development during adolescence. Developmental theorists attribute the onset of identity exploration to the increased desire for autonomy as children develop. Prior to adolescence, children's identities are inextricably tied to those of their primary caregivers. Most preadolescent children lack the necessary agency to make decisions about how their time is used, with whom they interact, and which social groups they prefer to engage with. Their identity, therefore, is closely tied to the significant adults in their lives, who are charged with making decisions about the aforementioned factors that will shape the child's identity as he or she progresses into adolescence. Over time, adolescents' reliance on adults to name their identities lessens and is exchanged for an increased dependence on peer groups. This sense of group loyalty typically results in youth becoming conformists. Head (2002) highlights the role of groups in influencing adolescents' choices in his study of high school students: "Members of a group wear similar clothes, enjoy the same music and support the same football clubs. The image of youth as independent pioneering spirits has little relevance at this stage" (p. 30). At this stage, identity is simultaneously defined by sameness (adherence to group loyalty) and difference (the extent to which adherence to group loyalty signifies an incongruence with other social groups) (Erikson, 1968).

Multiple theories are designed to provide insight into the development of identity during adolescence. Erikson's (1968) foundational work on identity development speaks to the fluidity of identity. Adolescents "try on" several identities throughout their development before settling on an identity that will carry them into adulthood (Erikson, 1968; Longest, 2009). Erikson's notion of "trying on" identities is less about exploration and more closely connected to the need for peer approval prevalent in the developmental stage of adolescence. As they attempt to find acceptance and recognition from peers, adolescents respond to their identity crises by redefining themselves (Longest, 2009). Erikson describes this process as "the persistent adolescent endeavor to define, overdefine, and redefine themselves" (p. 87). This theory, therefore, presumes that adolescents change their identity because of a personal desire, leaving little room for social predictors in explaining identity movement (Longest, 2009).

Erikson's identity theory is characterized by simultaneous reflection on oneself and observation of communal culture. "In psychological terms, identity formation employs a process of simultaneous reflection and observation, a process taking place on all levels of mental functioning, by which the individual judges himself in the light of what he perceives to be the way in which others judge him" (Erikson, 1968, p. 22).

Erikson's theory assumes young people can claim any identity they choose, but we know from experience that this is not always true. Peers play a significant role in controlling who is allowed to take on particular identities, and even if a student wants to change identities, they may be unable to do so. Identity, therefore, is often less about choice; rather, adolescents are segregated into different identities based on their ability to conform to established norms.

Social Identity. Social identity is based on the idea that individuals define themselves, at least in part, by the groups to which they belong and by the social categories that are important to them. While individual identity focuses on the unique aspects of an individual, social identity emphasizes the commonalities and connections individuals share with others in specific social groups. Cohen (2022) uses the backseat driver as a metaphor for social identity:

> When we identify with a group, it's as though we're driving with an insistent backseat driver, urging us what to do, where to turn, what to look out for, and how to handle other drivers. Because we want to belong to our group, we have a strong tendency to follow these directives, which are often unspoken, taking the form of norms that we learn the group endorses. (p. 58)

In addition to knowing the norms and expectations of their groups, students are acutely aware of the continuum of social identities and how each moves closer to or away from dominant social identities. One of the most recognized aspects of adolescent life is the presence of social identity groups in schools, such as jocks, preps, or punks. Although this notion of social identity is based on students' construction of group identity, it illustrates the cultural capital associated with being a member of the ingroup. Further, the stratification of students in this well-known and implicitly accepted caste system is further compounded when it intersects with racial and/or sexual identities.

There is a significant gap in research regarding how race, gender, and sexuality influence social identity groups in schools (Harrison, 2015). The absence of race, gender, and sexuality suggests that individuals can detach themselves from their inherited identities when joining social groups. Additionally, it implies that these factors do not actively impact social identity groups or affect how adolescents enter or leave the aforementioned groups. The exclusion of race, gender, and sexuality from the discourse on social identity groups highlights the need for further investigation into how these intersecting factors influence group identities. Specifically, there is a need to uncover the experiences of marginalized adolescents with multiple and conflicting identities. By uncovering these unheard stories, similar to counternarratives, we can amplify the voices of marginalized individuals and challenge our own perceptions of reality.

MARGINALIZED GROUP IDENTITY

Marginalized group identity refers to the collective identity and experiences of individuals belonging to social groups systematically disadvantaged or oppressed in a society. These groups have limited access to power, resources, opportunities, and social privileges compared to dominant groups. Marginalized identities include race, ethnicity, gender, sexual orientation, socioeconomic status, disability, religion, or immigration status, and they often intersect, leading to unique experiences of marginalization (intersectionality). People in marginalized groups are aware of facing discrimination, prejudice, stigmatization, or exclusion based on societal norms and biases.

Understanding marginalized group identity can be enhanced by examining racial identity models like Cross's developmental theory of nigrescence (McKoy, 2013) and the multidimensional model of racial identity (MMRI) (Sellers et al., 1998). These models describe stages through which Black adolescents progress in developing their racial identity, acknowledging the significance of race and dealing with racism's impacts. MMRI examines perceptions of race and its integration into Black identity, considering dimensions such as racial salience, centrality, regard, and ideology.

Both theories focus on race but can assist in understanding social identity development in marginalized groups and promoting antioppressive education. They recognize the hierarchical structure created by dominant groups within White patriarchal societies, leading to the devaluation of marginalized groups. However, marginalized group identity is not solely defined by victimhood; it also serves as a basis for collective mobilization, advocacy, and social justice pursuit. It fosters community, resilience, and empowerment, providing strength and support to challenge oppressive systems and strive for equality and inclusivity.

Oppositional Social Identity. Oppositional social identity is a form of resistance from assimilation into dominant culture. Resistance can be defined as opposition with a social and political purpose. This oppositional social identity serves as a means of protection from psychological assault of dominant group oppression and keeps the dominant group at a distance. Tatum's (1997) example of Black students' resistance and rejection of White norms shows how oppositional social identity impacts ideology and behavior: "Certain styles of speech, dress, and music, for example, may be embraced as 'authentically Black' and become highly valued, while attitudes and behaviors associated with Whites are viewed with disdain" (p. 61). Abowitz (2000) studied a group of West Indian males that formed an oppositional social identity to resist the White middle-class norms of their high school, which they perceived as irrelevant: "These students construct an identity of style (clothing, body decoration, attitude) and action (speaking patois around teachers who cannot understand the language, cutting class, yelling at teachers, breaking many school rules) to oppose school authority" (p. 881). Abowitz notes that although these two social groups—West Indian males and White middle-class authority—clash, they both remain fundamentally unchanged by the interactions.

The creation of oppositional social identities as resistance is not exclusive to racialized identities. For minority identities, such as non-heterosexuals, ingroups are formed by persons who are likely to suffer the same deprivations because they share the same stigma—fellow sufferers—as opposed to people who do not share that stigma—the outgroup. In fact, there is a growing population of students who resist the societal norms determined by dominant groups. Shapiro (2005) recognizes the prevalence of oppositional social identities in all schools, describing students who "resist the behaviors, attitudes, and appearance of the student mainstream . . . [and] create, through their own dress, language, and rituals, a subculture of style that violates the institutional norms" (p. 168). According to Solórzano and Bernal (2001), resistance theories demonstrate the ways in which individuals negotiate and struggle with social structures and create meaning from these interactions. They critique traditional perceptions of student resistance, which often interpret students' behavior as disruptive and lacking any critique of the social conditions to which they are responding. But what if we allowed ourselves to interpret students' behavior differently?

Assimilation and Negotiation. Students' need for acceptance is not solely related to their marginalized identity group; there is also a desire to find acceptance from dominant groups. Similar to the ways in which adolescents "perform" in ways that "fit" the accepted norms of their oppositional social identity group, they also develop conforming strategies to gain acceptance from dominant social groups. A common strategy is assimilation. Assimilation involves the forfeit of identity groups eschewed by the dominant culture in an effort to conform to White, male, Christian, heterosexual, middle-class standards (Purpel, 2000).

But assimilation into the dominant group by de-emphasizing characteristics that might identify an individual with a marginalized group comes at a cost. While there may be some benefits from the perceived kinship with the dominant group, there is an increased risk of psychological isolation and feelings of depression for students who are rejected by their marginalized identity group for their desire to assimilate and who are not fully accepted by the dominant identity group. While assimilation focuses on the process of adopting the cultural norms and values of a dominant group, identity negotiation pertains to the dynamic interaction between an individual's self-identity and the expectations and influences of their social environment.

Identity negotiation occurs when individuals encounter situations or environments where their identities are relevant and may come into question or conflict. This process can be influenced by factors such as cultural norms, social expectations, personal values, and the power dynamics present within a given context.

During identity negotiation, individuals may engage in introspection, self-reflection, and self-questioning to explore and make sense of their own beliefs, values, interests, and experiences. They also consider how these aspects align with or differ from the expectations and norms of the social groups or contexts they find themselves in.

The relationship between assimilation and identity negotiation lies in the way individuals from minority or marginalized groups navigate their identities in the context of assimilation pressures. While assimilation may involve conforming to dominant norms and expectations, identity negotiation allows individuals to critically reflect on the impact of assimilation on their self-identity. It involves examining the extent to which assimilation compromises or enhances one's sense of self, authenticity, and connection to their original culture or group. It can involve selectively adopting certain aspects of the dominant culture while maintaining or reinterpreting elements of their original culture. Identity negotiation provides a space for individuals to negotiate their identities, reconcile conflicts, and assert their unique cultural and social perspectives.

Assimilators and identity negotiators can tell you a lot about the culture and climate of your school. They can provide a window into the hierarchies of social identity and highlight which social identities carry the most social capital. Harrison (2015) recounts the stories of Black men who identify as same gender loving (SGL) as they negotiated their marginalized identities during their K–12 experiences: "Stephen described his identity negotiation as an ongoing internal conversation with himself. As he was interacting with others, he reminded himself how to craft his identity performance based on his audience: Depending on who was around, I would tell myself, 'Don't give them too much. Don't be too flamboyant. Don't give them too much. Don't be too Black'" (p. 143). Like Stephen, Tony had a similar inner dialogue that helped him "read the room" and make adjustments to his identity performance based on who was present. While their identity negotiation stories highlight their ability to anticipate how they will likely be received in every new situation and with every new audience, their stories provide a window into which social identities are viewed as the most desirable and which carry the most social capital. Further, these stories can help us gain a better understanding of how much a student's behavior is shaped by the context in which they are immersed.

SOCIAL HOMELESSNESS

In our ongoing pursuit of equity and improvement in education, it is crucial for educational leaders to understand and center the experiences of marginalized students. While student-centered approaches have gained recognition, there is a need to delve deeper and focus specifically on centering the experiences of socially homeless students who lack a sense of belonging. These students navigate multiple social identities, yet find themselves without a social group that fully embraces and validates their intersecting identities. When belonging is absent, it gives us insight into the conditions that foster belonging. By shining a light on the concept of social homelessness, we can gain insights into the challenges faced by these students and explore strategies to support their sense of belonging.

Harrison (2009) metaphorically extends the notion of "home" as a representation of identity and belonging. He defines social homelessness as the state in which individuals with multiple social identities lack a social group to which they can fully belong. One might assume that having membership in several groups would provide options for finding a social home, but on closer examination, a nuanced situation emerges. It is the very membership in particular social groups that prevents belonging to any of them. Consequently, individuals find themselves caught in a conundrum: They must either mask certain aspects of themselves to conform to the desirable traits of a particular social group or face social homelessness by remaining true to themselves.

In his qualitative study on the phenomenon of social homelessness, Harrison (2015) interviewed adult Black males who identify as SGL about their K–12 experiences, as previously mentioned. As African American SGL males are a part of two marginalized identity groups, they have an increased risk of experiencing social homelessness. This heightened risk is not only because they are a part of more than one marginalized group; rather, it is because of the bifurcated nature of their racial and sexual identities. As they recounted their experiences, social homelessness was often discussed in terms of feeling like an outsider, both as an outsider because of racial identity and an outsider because of sexual identity. In the following excerpts, we highlight the unique challenges experienced by one of the socially homeless students featured in the study:

> Jonah Curry is a 25-year-old male who recognizes the uniqueness of his life experiences. He is a first-generation African American who was raised by his Nigerian father and was one of two Black students at his K–8 White Catholic school in a North Carolina suburb. Jonah's family was religious and in addition to daily mass at school, he and his family regularly attended a nearby church on Sundays. His younger sister was the other Black student in his school, and he eventually learned to be comfortable as the racial minority in school. In high school, Jonah attended a public school that was racially and economically diverse. The demographics of his high school represented the small town in which he was raised. (pp. 81–82)
>
> Although his experience related to feeling like an outsider with Black peers, Jonah also discussed his inability to fit in. All throughout elementary and middle school, Jonah attended White Catholic schools. Although he was a good student who worked hard in class and took his education seriously, Jonah felt like an outcast in elementary and middle school: "Whenever things went wrong [in school], people always looked at me." Early on, Jonah said that being African American was difficult for him because he was surrounded by White faces all his life. Jonah yearned for more relationships with African American students. He felt that those relationships would help to define him and make him feel more comfortable. Unfortunately, Jonah's wish for feeling like an insider went unfulfilled when he matriculated to a diverse high school with a large population of African American students: "I never fit in . . . and even when I should have fit in, I didn't." (p. 102)
>
> After attending predominately White schools in elementary and middle school, Jonah Curry attended his neighborhood's public high school whose

demographics better represented the diversity of his southern, suburban town and included a significant number of African American students. "I tried to hang out with the students I thought I wanted to be with all my life and that didn't work out either because those kids didn't, I wasn't like them. I didn't grow up in the same environments as they did so they didn't accept me as I thought they would because they felt I acted 'White' or spoke 'White' or other things" (p. 145). Although he was excited to see students that looked like him when he got to high school, Jonah was not accepted by his African American peers and found the difficulty of not fitting in with the Black community to be a painful experience.

After grappling with the alienation he felt from African American students during his freshman year, Jonah felt that he had little to lose and he decided to come out of the closet. While his choice to act "White" and be openly gay provided him with acceptance from his White peers, he continued to struggle with the pain of not being "Black" enough to be accepted by African American students. Once Jonah came out to his peers and felt accepted by other gay students, he was faced with a new hierarchy within the homosexual male community of his school. This hierarchy privileged Whiteness over Blackness and masculinity over femininity. Although Jonah was effeminate, he wasn't seen as one of the "flamboyant queens" he avoided. Jonah feared that the association with gay people, particularly flamboyantly gay people, would open him up to verbal and/ or physical abuse from his friends. After Jonah's friends would bully the flamboyant queens, they would reassure him of their friendship by saying, "Okay, he's a [f-slur], but Jonah, you're not like that." Similarly, Jonah's White friends would also say things like, "I hate when [n-words] do this or that. Jonah, they should be more like you. You're a nice Black guy." While Jonah's choice to act "White" initially provided him with the space to embrace his sexuality, it did not protect him from further discrimination based on his racial or sexual identities. (p. 146)

Jonah's story highlights the complexities of negotiating multiple marginalized identities, especially when those identities are competing with each other. Outside of a couple of teachers who provided him with unsolicited support, Jonah felt alone and did not believe that the adults understood how he was feeling. Based on our experience as school leaders, Jonah was probably correct. As leaders, we are programmed to respond to challenges with fixes. Often this predilection for solutions causes us to rush to action and miss the nuances of the stories we collect. In his initial comments at the start of the interview, Jonah described his K–12 school experiences as fun. However, as he began to tell the stories that punctuated his experiences, it was clear that it wasn't fun. Toward the end of the interview when he reflects on what was missing from his schooling experience, Jonah talked about his contemplation of suicide.

Safir and Dugan (2021) cite deep listening as a core stance for school transformation, but do we really know what to listen for? Do we know how to make meaning of the stories that are shared? As expected, several of the participants in Harrison's (2015) study highlighted the negative ways they coped with social homelessness. However, among the stories of substance abuse, aggression, and alienation were examples of positive actions— actions that we typically ascribe to students who are thriving:

> Based on this theoretical model of social homelessness, students may respond to the feelings associated with social homelessness by engaging in high academic work and/or taking on student leadership roles. Within the master-narrative of schools, successful students—those who excel academically or hold school offices—view the climate of their school as positive and are receiving the adult support they need to excel. Because of the positive attributes of academic achievement and student leadership, it is very easy for principals to overlook the negative feelings of alienation, shame and lack of acceptance that may be a catalyst to these behaviors. Specifically, if students are engaging in high academic work to fill the void they are experiencing by being socially homeless, it is likely that they will require additional support for their emotional well-being. Similarly, this theoretical model and the experiences shared in this study show that multi-marginalized students may respond to their social homelessness with a quest for popularity. Within the master narrative of schools, popular students are viewed as having it all together and are therefore at risk of not getting the emotional support needed to address their feelings of inferiority. In the current study, the more oppressed, marginalized and ostracized participants felt, the more important it was to feel validated via "normalizing offices." Normalizing offices describes those traditional positions in school that play significant roles in the master-narrative of school (e.g. homecoming king, SGA president, jock, etc.). Solórzano and Yosso (2002) note that research and theoretical models that seek to explain the inequities in education and the gaps in academic achievement often support majoritarian viewpoints through the constant amplification of deficits. The theoretical model presented in this study nuances the ways in which multi-marginalized students respond to their social homelessness, highlights the potentiality of positive responses to social homelessness and promotes the use of counter-narratives to expose deficit informed research that silences and distorts the epistemologies of multi-marginalized students. (Solórzano & Yosso, 2002) (pp. 179–180)

The implications of social homelessness within an educational context are significant, particularly for school leaders. Multi-marginalized students, who navigate the intersectionality of multiple marginalized identities, often find themselves socially homeless within the school community. Their unique experiences and perspectives are overlooked by the dominant narratives that shape the school's climate, perpetuating an incomplete understanding of the educational landscape. To address this, school leaders must problematize the master-narrative within their schools. The master-narrative, which typically reflects the experiences and opinions of dominant identity groups, can inadvertently marginalize multi-marginalized students. It is crucial to recognize that the dominant narrative is not a universal truth and may overshadow the realities of socially homeless students.

Centering students requires us to slow down our thinking and to acknowledge that we tend to have more confidence in our ability to read people than we should. Frequently, due to our confidence in understanding and reading others, we neglect to inquire about their thoughts and emotions. This missed opportunity could result in significant revelations that foster stronger connections. Using this notion of social homelessness as a lens for a more nuanced understanding of students' experiences requires empathy.

EMPATHY AND EMPATHY INTERVIEWS

Empathy, also known as being empathetic, involves two essential aspects: understanding someone else's perspective and recognizing their emotions (Zaki & Ochsner, 2012). Before exploring empathy's role in improvement science and equity, it's crucial to first consider the experience of being empathized with. This highlights the positive impact of empathy before discussing its application in creating fairer systems. Empathy goes beyond understanding marginalized students' experiences; it also fosters respect, connection, a sense of belonging, and psychological safety (Morelli et al., 2015). Conversely, feeling misunderstood leads to isolation and alienation (Cohen, 2022; Harrison, 2015).

Understanding someone else's viewpoint is a cognitive activity involving considering their values, beliefs, and experiences and letting go of our own biases to understand how they perceive the world (Goldman, 2012). However, several cognitive features lead us to overestimate our understanding of others. First, we have an egocentric bias, defaulting to see the world from our own perspective. We tend to think events are more about us than they are and that others pay more attention to us than they actually do (Zuckerman, 1979). Second, we rely on cues like tone of voice and body language to interpret emotions. Indeed, there is now a whole language of digital communication via emoji that seeks to convey what words in an email cannot—tone and affect—that relies on a shared understanding of what a winking emoji means, or a happy face, or an eyeroll. But these caricatures of emotion do not correspond with the actual relationship between facial expression and body language with emotion, which is actually very limited (Barrett, 2017).

Empathy has long been used in design to understand users and meet their needs effectively. In medicine, empathy is crucial for better patient outcomes, and research shows it reduces the risk of suicide attempts and improves recovery from suicidal episodes. Empathy in education should draw from both the design and medical perspectives. Viewing empathy as a skill rather than a trait is essential, especially when centering the experiences of marginalized students. By acknowledging empathy as a learnable skill, educators can intentionally cultivate it within themselves and their students, creating an inclusive and supportive learning environment. This shift in perspective highlights the urgency of prioritizing empathy in education for the benefit of all students, promoting equity, emotional well-being, and social cohesion (Trzeciak & Mazzarelli, 2019).

Empathy Interviews. Safir and Dugan (2021) describe empathy interviews as a cornerstone for design thinking that helps us not only listen for how a person feels but also to uncover how they perceive the equity challenges we are trying to address. In addition to serving as a data collection tool for unearthing stories from the margins, empathy interviews serve as a powerful tool in building leaders' empathy skills by providing a structured and intentional approach to understanding the perspectives and experiences of others. In an empathy interview, the interviewer engages in active listening and open-ended questioning to gain insight into the emotions, needs, and challenges faced by individuals. Through these interviews, leaders immerse themselves in the lived experiences of their students, fostering a deeper connection and appreciation for their unique journeys.

By stepping into the shoes of others and actively seeking to understand their stories, leaders cultivate a heightened sense of empathy, transcending a surface-level understanding of empathy as mere sympathy or benevolence. Empathy interviews push leaders to set aside their assumptions and preconceptions, creating a space where genuine human connection can flourish. This empathetic perspective enables leaders to make more informed and compassionate decisions, tailor support and resources to the specific needs of their team members, and create inclusive environments where everyone's voices are heard and valued.

Moreover, empathy interviews promote a culture of trust and psychological safety within the organization. When leaders demonstrate a sincere commitment to centering students' experiences, individuals feel seen, respected, and understood. Leaders who prioritize empathy through such interviews inspire others to emulate these behaviors, fostering a ripple effect of empathy throughout the organization and beyond.

We end this section on a note of caution. Empathy interviews are a wonderful tool, and we advocate for their use. But the stakes are a little different for interviewer versus interviewee. For the interviewer, the empathy interview can be viewed as a box to be checked, a step in a process, or a simple source of useful information. For the interviewee, however, the empathy interview has much more potential to be a source of connection and a foundation for belonging. Trzeciak and Mazzarelli report research that shows that doctors routinely miss emotional cues from their patients and miss 60% to 90% of opportunities to respond compassionately to something the patient says. The corollary of this is that the patient experiences an event that might have been affirming and supportive as distancing and clinical. We hope, therefore, that educators who are planning on using empathy interviews understand them to be more than simply a source of data. With careful planning and implementation, the empathy interview will be more than a one-way flow of information; the interviewer will respond as well as receive and will be well-practiced in the listening stance and skills we describe in Chapter 8.

FOCUS GROUPS

Recently, we were asked by a district partner to conduct focus groups with middle school students. The aim was to understand their perspectives on equity in the district. During the discussions, students shared stories of how marginalized students were being teased and excluded. Although students adhered to the rule that they couldn't name others as victims or perpetrators, the stories were familiar, and they knew the people involved. As the discussions unfolded, we could see some students grappling with the realization that some of their friends—people who they saw as "good kids"—could engage in such divisive behavior.

We analyzed the data and identified 33 codes representing common themes. These themes fell into five categories: Climate, Microaggressions, Macroaggressions, Student Behavior, and Teachers. As we delved into Climate, the theme of Entertainment emerged. Students said their peers engaged in negative behavior because they wanted to be funny. Some admitted to doing hurtful things to entertain their friends. Interestingly, many entertainers identified themselves as part of marginalized groups. This highlighted the strong need for belonging among students. Being funny was seen as a way to fit in and increase their sense of belonging, even for those who felt marginalized.

These examples as well as others that emerged in the data highlighted the need to address individual student behavior, while also fostering an equitable school climate in which students see the behaviors described earlier as problematic instead of entertaining. While school leaders were aware of many of the stories shared and recognized the need to address individual bad actors, they had not considered the role of the audience. The focus groups gave the administrators a new perspective to consider as they worked collaboratively with students, staff, and families to address the school's climate. As they considered change ideas to improve the climate, they prioritized those that would address individual students while also addressing the audience. Instead of simply asking, "How can we stop students from targeting their marginalized peers?" they also asked, "How can we shift from a bystanding climate where students are entertained by the belittling of their peers to an upstanding climate in which students are willing to intervene and promote positive peer pressure?" This was not the first time administrators asked students about their experiences. This school, like most we work with, administers a climate survey to students, staff, and families each year. But the surveys didn't provide the actionable and nuanced data they received from the focus groups.

Focus groups as a qualitative research method hold the power to transcend mere data collection and become a transformative tool for centering the experiences of marginalized students in education. Beyond the traditional approach of gathering information, focus groups offer a safe and supportive space for students to share their personal stories, perspectives, and lived experiences. In this process, they find their voices amplified, their perspectives valued, and their unique challenges acknowledged.

In the context of improvement science and equity, focus groups play a crucial role in uncovering the nuances of students' journeys and understanding the complex web of barriers they face. These groups go beyond surface-level data to delve into the lived realities of students, fostering empathy, understanding, and a deeper connection between educators and learners. The significance of focus groups lies not only in their ability to inform equitable interventions and policies but also in their capacity to create a sense of belonging and solidarity among marginalized students. By bringing together students with shared experiences, focus groups create a supportive community where students find comfort in knowing they are not alone in their struggles and triumphs.

In the middle school focus groups described earlier, students who had been targeted because of their marginalized identities were comforted by peers who shared similar experiences. Further, students who had previously been perpetrators gained a better understanding of the impact of their actions and discussed the challenges of letting go of the cultural capital given to the school's entertainers. In this case, the focus groups were more than a process for gathering information and centering marginalized students' experiences. They also served as an initial step in moving toward the creation of a more equitable learning environment for all students.

Through focus groups, educators become active participants in students' stories, moving beyond a one-sided approach and embracing a culture of listening and empathy. As students share their experiences, educators gain insights into the challenges students face, their unique needs, and the strengths they bring to the educational setting. This reciprocal sharing fosters mutual respect, trust, and a sense of agency among students, empowering them to be active contributors in shaping their educational journey.

While continuous improvement and equity may seem like disparate fields, focus groups bridge the gap between the two, revealing their mutual attraction and complementarity. As Brandi Hinnant Crawford (2020) aptly points out, iterative change is a key component in the pursuit of justice and equality. Focus groups, with their iterative nature, provide a framework for reviewing and revising strategies to achieve equitable outcomes. In this way, they serve as a catalyst for change, propelling both improvement science and equity work forward.

AT YOUR DESK OR IN THE HALLS

Understanding individual and social identity development, the nuances of marginalized identity development, and the unique challenges faced by socially homeless students equips leaders with the necessary tools to comprehend students' lived experiences more deeply and gain a clearer understanding of the systems that produce the outcomes we wish to improve. The integration of empathy interviews and focus groups into the fabric of educational leadership practices offers a profound opportunity to center the experiences of marginalized students. Beyond serving as data collection tools, empathy interviews and focus groups become transformative spaces where students can share their lived experiences, hear each other's stories, and find solidarity. By centering the experiences of marginalized students, we gain critical insights to inform equitable interventions and policies. This journey requires openness to iterative change and a commitment to fostering a culture of trust, belonging, and continuous improvement. By prioritizing empathy and centering students' voices, we can forge a path toward compassionate, inclusive, and equitable educational environments where all students can thrive.

Reflection Questions

- How can I deepen my understanding of individual and social identities, including marginalized identity, to better interpret and relate to students' lived experiences?
- In what ways can I actively listen to multi-marginalized students, acknowledging their sense of social homelessness and the challenges they face in finding belonging and acceptance?
- How can I create a safe and supportive space for multi-marginalized students to share their intersecting identities, articulate their struggles, and seek validation?
- How can I use my empathetic understanding of students' experiences to inform policies and practices that promote inclusion and equity for all students, especially those at the margins?

CHAPTER 3

Dispositions of the Liberatory Improver

In a bustling neighborhood nestled between city skyscrapers, one school stood out not just for its academic achievements but also for its sense of community and belonging. This haven of learning was led by Dr. Michelle Sneed, a visionary educator whose leadership style resonated deeply with the students and staff.

Michelle's story began long before she became a principal. Growing up in a similar neighborhood, she had experienced firsthand the challenges and adversities that many of her students faced. While Michelle had been described by her teachers as a joy to teach, her younger sister Regina struggled to find her place in school. After the unexpected death of their mother, Regina began acting out, and the school's focus on her behavior overshadowed their focus on her learning. Sadly, her academic performance confirmed Regina's beliefs that school wasn't for her. In high school, Michelle and Regina would spend hours at the kitchen table working on assignments and discussing the lessons of the day. Rather than showing what she knew in class the next day, Regina would sit silently in class hoping to be left alone. Despite their best efforts, Regina ended her high school career as soon as she was old enough to drop out.

Michelle knew that her sister had the ability to be successful in school, and over time, she became frustrated by the teachers' deficit mindset and hyperfocus on what Regina was unable to do. So, she decided to become an educator. Michelle's goal was to be the teacher that Regina needed, one with a deep sense of empathy and a whatever-it-takes mentality. Her journey from a small apartment to the classroom and then to the principal's office wasn't just about climbing the professional ladder; it was a transformative quest to uplift the lives of those she served and led with empathy.

Every morning, rain or shine, Michelle stood at the entrance of the school, greeting students as they entered. The warm smile on her face and the twinkle in her eyes communicated a simple message: "You are seen. You are valued." She knew the names of every student, their interests, and even their struggles. This wasn't just a formality for her; it was a genuine connection that set the tone for the entire school day. Inside the school, the walls were adorned with colorful artwork and inspirational quotes. The class-rooms were lively spaces where engaged students collaborated on projects that aligned with their interests. Teachers, too, felt the impact of Michelle's leadership. She fostered an environment of trust, empowering teachers to explore innovative teaching methods and tailor their approaches to the diverse needs of their students.

One particular incident demonstrated Michelle's deep empathy and its influence on her leadership. A few years back, a student named Alexis joined the school. Alexis was quiet and reserved, often retreating into the background during classroom discussions—a practice she recognized from Regina. Instead of labeling Alexis as disinterested or aloof, Michelle took the time to understand the underlying reasons for this behavior.

Through conversations with Alexis's parents and teachers, Michelle learned that Alexis had recently lost a close family member and was struggling to cope with the grief. Armed with this knowledge, Michelle worked with Alexis's teachers to provide extra support and a safe space for sharing feelings. She also connected Alexis with a peer mentor who had faced a similar loss. Over time, Alexis began to open up, and the transformation was remarkable. The once-withdrawn student became a vibrant participant in class discussions and extracurricular activities.

Michelle's empathetic leadership wasn't confined to the walls of the school. She forged strong partnerships with local community organizations, leveraging their resources to provide additional support to students and families. From after-school programs to food drives, her commitment to holistic student well-being extended beyond academics. As the years passed, the school's reputation grew, not just for its academic achievements but also for its inclusive and nurturing environment. Parents spoke of the positive changes they witnessed in their children, and teachers lauded Michelle's supportive leadership.

Michelle's story is a testament to the ways in which our dispositions shape our leadership actions. While her focus on empathy was informed by her experiences with her younger sister, she made a conscious decision to adopt empathy as one of the dispositions that would guide her actions as a leader. Grounding her leadership moves in empathy, Michelle developed systems and routines that allowed her to prioritize relationships, understand the needs of others, and foster an environment of trust and support. And while she never explicitly claimed that her dispositions shaped her actions, the impact of her empathetic leadership spoke volumes. The school she led wasn't just a place of education; it was a community of care, collaboration, and transformation.

This chapter is not about convincing you to lead with empathy like Michelle. Instead, it is an invitation to think about the dispositions that you have adopted and reflect on how they shape who you are as a leader. Elsewhere in this book we have pointed out that, despite impressions to the contrary, improvement is not about tools—it's about people and relationships. Describing the dispositions of educators engaged in equity-focused improvement, therefore, is a crucial endeavor. In this chapter, we explore the set of dispositions that characterize liberatory improvers—equity-focused improvers who employ improvement science tools and processes in the service of social justice and equitable outcomes for students. And just as Michelle made a conscious choice to ground her leadership in empathy, we invite you to adopt the dispositions discussed in this chapter that are associated with challenging oppressive systems, empowering marginalized voices, and focusing on systematic improvement that leads to true transformation. Drawing on research and scholarship from inside and outside the fields of equity and improvement science, we construct a list of dispositions that captures the essence of equity-focused leaders using improvement science as a means of advancing social justice in schools and districts. These dispositions form the foundation of liberatory improvement science leadership, guiding practitioners toward practices that foster inclusivity, challenge oppressive systems, and empower marginalized communities.

BACKGROUND ON DISPOSITIONS

So, what even are dispositions? Situated somewhere between personality traits, mindsets, and skills, dispositions represent more than attributes or abilities—they are a way of being. Our identity becomes intertwined with our embrace of these dispositions. They shape the lens through which we view the world, influencing our thoughts, actions, and interactions. In academic literature, the crucial role of dispositions in shaping educational experiences and outcomes is examined. Scholars often delve into the complex interplay between dispositions, learning environments, and educational practices, recognizing the profound impact these dispositions have on students, educators, and leaders alike. Through this lens, dispositions are not static elements, but rather dynamic qualities that evolve and develop over time, calling for intentional cultivation and nurturing within educational settings.

To start our conversation, we draw inspiration from Perkins et al. (1993), who discussed the concept of dispositions and identified three key elements: inclinations, sensitivities, and abilities. Now, these elements are not separate categories, but rather intertwined aspects, so we'll consider them as useful guidelines rather than rigid divisions. According to Perkins and his team, inclination refers to a person's internal desire to engage in a specific behavior. Sensitivity, on the other hand, involves being aware of situations where a particular type of behavior is appropriate. To illustrate, someone who is sensitive to the importance of open-minded thinking will notice instances where narrow thinking, prejudice, and bias might be prevalent and where open-mindedness is needed (Perkins et al., 1993). Finally, ability refers to a person's competence in carrying out the actions they are inclined to undertake. For example, to practice open-mindedness, one must possess the fundamental capacity to see things from multiple perspectives, have the inclination to invest energy in doing so, and be able to identify suitable opportunities to actively listen and embrace alternative viewpoints (Biag & Scherer, 2021).

Leadership dispositions are all about the natural qualities and tendencies that individuals have, which influence how they act as leaders. These dispositions are considered stable characteristics that shape leaders' thoughts, emotions, and behaviors in different situations. As our understanding of leadership has evolved over time, so has the research on leadership dispositions.

In the past, leadership theories mainly focused on pinpointing specific traits that set effective leaders apart from nonleaders. This approach, known as the trait theory of leadership, assumed that certain inherent qualities predisposed individuals to be successful leaders. For example, early trait theorists like Carlyle (1841) and Stogdill (1948) suggested that traits such as intelligence, self-confidence, determination, and sociability were important for effective leadership. However, the trait theory faced criticism for its inability to consistently identify a definitive set of leadership traits. Over time, researchers shifted their focus to other aspects of leadership, including behaviors and situational factors. This led to the development of behavioral and contingency theories, which highlighted that leadership effectiveness depends on the interaction between leader traits and the situation at hand.

In recent years, there has been a renewed interest in studying leadership dispositions, with a particular emphasis on understanding the underlying psychological processes that shape leadership behaviors. Researchers have explored various dispositions, such as emotional intelligence, self-efficacy, locus of control, resilience, ethical orientation, and openness to experience.

Wilson et al. (2020) present a comprehensive framework for understanding leadership dispositions and how they can be developed. The authors propose a model that encompasses four key domains: intrapersonal, interpersonal, cognitive, and ethical. Within each domain, they identify specific dispositions like self-awareness, empathy, critical thinking, and integrity. The authors argue that leadership dispositions are not fixed traits, but can be nurtured and grown through intentional practice and reflection. They emphasize the importance of experiential learning, mentoring, and self-reflection in developing leadership dispositions. Further, they provide valuable insights into the theoretical foundations of leadership dispositions and offer practical implications for leadership development programs.

When discussing the dispositions of equity leaders, it's important to understand the distinctions between characteristics, traits, and dispositions. While these terms are sometimes used interchangeably, they have different connotations:

- Characteristics: Characteristics refer to the distinguishing features or qualities of a person. They can include physical attributes, such as height or eye color, as well as more abstract qualities like intelligence or creativity. Characteristics tend to describe inherent or relatively stable attributes of an individual.
- Traits: Traits are enduring personal qualities or attributes that influence a person's behavior, attitudes, and patterns of thinking. They are often considered relatively stable and consistent across different situations. Examples of traits could include empathy, perseverance, or conscientiousness. Traits are thought to be relatively innate but can also be developed and influenced by experiences.
- Dispositions: Dispositions are tendencies, inclinations, or prevailing attitudes that guide a person's actions and responses in specific situations. They represent a person's underlying predispositions or prevailing orientations. Dispositions can encompass a range of attitudes, beliefs, values, and orientations toward certain behaviors or circumstances. In the context of equity leadership, dispositions might include a commitment to fairness, inclusivity, empathy, and a willingness to challenge and address systemic inequities.

DISPOSITIONS IN IMPROVEMENT SCIENCE

In the realm of improvement science, the focus extends beyond the mere adoption of tools, protocols, and templates. It delves into the deeper beliefs and practices that underpin the work of effective improvers. These underlying dispositions, often referred to as "below-the-green-line" beliefs and improvement habits, form the bedrock of successful improvement efforts. When combined with a focus on equity, they become catalysts for transformative change in education.

Below-the-green-line beliefs encompass the fundamental mindsets and perspectives that drive improvement work. These beliefs recognize the complexity of educational systems and acknowledge the need for continuous learning and adaptation. Instead of seeking quick fixes or one-size-fits-all solutions, improvers with below-the-green-line beliefs embrace the notion that improvement is an ongoing journey that requires deep engagement and collaboration with stakeholders.

One important disposition in improvement science is the belief in the power of data. Effective improvers understand that data are not just a static set of numbers but a valuable resource for uncovering patterns, identifying root causes, and making informed decisions. In education, this can manifest as data literacy, where educators have the skills to analyze and interpret data to inform instructional practices and drive improvement. For example, an equity-focused improver might utilize disaggregated student achievement data to identify achievement gaps and develop targeted interventions that address the unique needs of marginalized student groups.

Another critical improvement habit is the commitment to collaboration and collective responsibility. Improvement efforts in education require the collective efforts of teachers, administrators, students, families, and community members. Equity-focused improvers recognize the importance of fostering a culture of collaboration where diverse voices are valued and actively sought. They engage in meaningful partnerships with stakeholders, ensuring that the experiences and perspectives of marginalized groups are centered in decision-making processes. For instance, an equity-focused improver might establish a teacher-led professional learning community that examines data, shares effective instructional strategies, and collectively designs interventions to address disparities in student outcomes.

Continuous learning and adaptation are central to the improvement mindset. Effective improvers embrace a growth-oriented outlook that encourages experimentation, learning from failures, and making iterative adjustments based on evidence and feedback. In the context of equity, this disposition becomes even more crucial. Equity-focused improvers understand that promoting social justice requires ongoing reflection and a commitment to dismantling systemic barriers. They are open to feedback, engage in critical self-reflection, and are willing to revise their approaches when faced with evidence of inequities. An example of this would be an equity-focused improver who analyzes discipline data and recognizes disproportionate disciplinary actions against students of color. In response, they develop restorative justice practices and engage in professional development to shift disciplinary practices toward a more equitable and supportive approach.

Below-the-green-line beliefs and improvement habits are not isolated concepts, but are intertwined and mutually reinforcing. They provide the foundation for effective improvement science, enabling educators to move beyond compliance-driven exercises and engage in purposeful, equity-focused improvement work. By combining these dispositions with a deep commitment to equity and social justice, educators can become powerful advocates for transforming schools into more inclusive, just, and equitable learning environments.

In the next section, we will explore the specific dispositions of equity leaders in education, further expanding our understanding of the qualities and characteristics that contribute to advancing equity and social justice within educational settings.

DISPOSITIONS OF EQUITY LEADERS IN EDUCATION

In the field of education, the work of equity leaders is paramount in addressing systemic inequities and advancing social justice within educational settings. These leaders possess a distinct set of dispositions that enable them to challenge the status quo, advocate for marginalized groups, and create inclusive learning environments. In this section, we will explore the specific dispositions of equity leaders in education; debunk the myth that these dispositions come naturally to Black, Indigenous, People of Color (BIPOC) or otherwise marginalized leaders; and discuss how these dispositions can be cultivated and nurtured in educators from all backgrounds.

Equity leaders demonstrate a critical consciousness, which involves an awareness of the historical and structural inequities that exist in society and the impact these have on educational opportunities. They possess a deep understanding of the root causes of disparities and actively challenge oppressive systems and practices. For example, an equity leader might analyze discipline data and recognize the disproportionate disciplinary actions taken against students of color. They use this awareness to advocate for restorative justice practices and alternative disciplinary approaches that promote fairness and equity.

Additionally, equity leaders value and embrace diverse cultures, languages, and experiences within the educational community. They cultivate cultural competence, which involves developing an understanding of and respect for different cultural norms, perspectives, and practices. This disposition enables them to create inclusive learning environments where all students feel valued and respected. An equity leader might collaborate with community organizations to integrate culturally responsive pedagogy into the curriculum, ensuring that students see their cultures reflected in their educational experiences.

Equity leaders possess a strong sense of empathy and a genuine concern for the well-being and success of all students. They actively seek to understand the experiences and challenges faced by marginalized students and communities. Through empathetic listening and engagement, they empower students, families, and educators to become agents of change. For instance, an equity leader might facilitate student-led initiatives that address social justice issues, providing opportunities for students to use their voices to advocate for equitable policies and practices.

Moreover, equity leaders demonstrate courage in advocating for equitable policies, practices, and resources within educational systems. They navigate complex power dynamics, challenge inequitable policies, and work to dismantle systemic barriers. For example, an equity leader might engage in policy advocacy to secure funding for high-quality early childhood education programs, recognizing the long-term impact of early interventions on closing achievement gaps.

It is essential to dispel the myth that the dispositions required for equity leadership come naturally to BIPOC or otherwise marginalized leaders. While personal experiences of inequity may provide motivation, the development of these dispositions requires intentional cultivation, learning, and ongoing self-reflection. The notion that these dispositions are exclusive to certain individuals perpetuates a deficit-based perspective, undermining the collective responsibility for equity held by all educators.

The cultivation and nurturing of these equity-focused dispositions should be a collective effort within educational communities. Educators from all backgrounds can develop these dispositions through intentional professional development, critical reflection, and collaboration. Schools and districts can create spaces for dialogue and learning, providing opportunities for educators to engage in culturally responsive teaching practices, examine implicit biases, and develop a critical understanding of the systems that perpetuate inequities.

Mentorship and coaching also play a crucial role in nurturing these dispositions. Established equity leaders can serve as mentors to support emerging leaders, sharing their experiences, strategies, and insights. By fostering a culture of learning and support, educational communities can create an environment that cultivates the dispositions necessary for equity-focused improvement work.

DISPOSITIONS OF LIBERATORY IMPROVERS

In Chapter 1 we introduced you to our concept of liberatory improvement, which offers a transformative approach that goes beyond traditional improvement efforts by centering the voices, perspectives, and agency of marginalized students and communities. Liberatory improvement calls for the intentional dismantling of oppressive systems and structures while striving to achieve equitable outcomes and experiences for all. While liberatory improvement is focused on improving equitable outcomes as the overarching goal of improvement, it is equally invested in democratizing the improvement process, ensuring that decision-making power is shared and distributed equitably among stakeholders, including students. It recognizes that those closest to the challenges and realities of education are best positioned to identify meaningful change ideas. Through active engagement, codesign, and shared decision-making, the voices of marginalized students and other stakeholders from the margins are valued and uplifted. This participatory approach acknowledges them as agents of their own liberation, affirming their expertise, knowledge, and lived experiences as valid and essential in shaping educational improvement initiatives. In this section, we will explore eight key dispositions that underpin liberatory improvement, empowering educators to become transformative leaders for equity.

1. Pragmatic Action. Liberatory improvers embody a disposition for pragmatic action because they understand that achieving equitable outcomes requires concrete and actionable steps. They recognize that it's not enough to simply talk about equity and justice; they must actively engage in evidence-based decision-making and implement strategies that lead to measurable improvements. These leaders proactively employ continuous improvement tools and methodologies to guide their efforts. They analyze data to identify the root causes of inequities and set specific, measurable goals driven by their exploration of the adjacent possible. They use evidence to inform their strategies, ensuring that their actions are grounded in both quantitative and qualitative data and research rather than relying solely on assumptions or personal biases.

As pragmatists, liberatory improvers prioritize the outcomes and results of educational practices. They focus on what actually works in practice and what benefits students the most, rather than being bound by rigid ideological dogmas that may not lead to positive outcomes. They understand that innovative solutions are not necessarily about chasing the newest and shiniest ideas, but rather about thinking and acting in new ways that are effective and meaningful for students. Through iterative cycles of improvement, liberatory improvers continuously monitor progress, adapt their approaches based on feedback and emerging insights, and drive sustained change. They are not afraid to course-correct if necessary and make adjustments based on the data they collect and the experiences of students and educators. This iterative process allows them to fine-tune their interventions and ensure that they are making a positive impact on marginalized students.

2. Critical Consciousness and Praxis. At the heart of liberatory improvement is critical consciousness and praxis. Critical consciousness refers to the ability to recognize and analyze the underlying power structures and inequalities in society. It involves developing an awareness of social, economic, and political issues and understanding how these issues affect different groups of people. Critical consciousness and praxis go beyond simply observing and accepting the status quo; they encourage individuals to question and challenge the prevailing norms, ideologies, and systems that perpetuate inequality and oppression. Assuming a critical stance in education is not about bashing schools or educators. It is born from a deep love of the institution of education and a deep faith in what it is able to accomplish in its best version. Therefore, the critique of the institution comes from the frustration of it not living up to its potential.

Critical consciousness and praxis also involve critically examining their own biases, assumptions, and privileges while developing a deep understanding of the historical and systemic inequities that exist within education.

But self-examination is not enough. By raising their consciousness, educators can challenge oppressive narratives, disrupt inequitable practices, and promote transformative change. These leaders possess a deep understanding of the historical and social contexts that perpetuate educational inequities. They critically examine power dynamics, biases, and structural barriers that marginalize students based on their race, gender, socioeconomic status, and other intersecting identities. The leadership moves that flow from this deep critical consciousness represent the praxis component of this disposition. By engaging in praxis—the reflective and transformative application of knowledge—they challenge oppressive systems, advocate for social justice, and enact systemic change. Liberatory improvers are not selfish with their critical consciousness and praxis. As leaders, they strive to foster critical thinking among stakeholders, encouraging others to critically analyze the root causes of inequities and actively participate in dismantling oppressive structures. Additionally, they develop systems and routines that challenge others to enact their critical consciousness in service of equity. Liberatory improvers know that understanding the system means understanding the lived experiences of people within the system. As a result, they center the lived experiences of stakeholders who have historically been silenced, seek out stories from the margins, and are intentional in gaining a better grasp on experiences of people who identify differently. For example, a liberatory improvement leader might engage in critical reflection on their school's discipline practices, recognize the disproportionate disciplinary actions against students from marginalized backgrounds, and explore the stories behind the quantitative data to uncover how White supremacy cultural expectations shape how students' behavior is interpreted.

3. Equity-Centered Collaboration. Equity-centered collaboration is a vital disposition for liberatory improvers. These leaders understand that achieving equity requires collective responsibility and collaboration among diverse stakeholders. They actively seek out and value diverse perspectives, ensuring that historically marginalized voices, including those of students, families, and community members, are heard and respected. Liberatory improvers create inclusive spaces for dialogue and foster trusting relationships based on mutual respect and shared decision-making. They recognize that in order for true collaboration to happen, leaders must focus their collaborative efforts and engage in buffering—protecting their work from the competing demands of the larger systems that often derail or complicate improvement efforts—and bridging—finding ways to connect their work to the demands of the larger system and overarching goals that represent the aspirations of the community (Yurkofsky et al., 2020).

As collaborators or co-conspirators, liberatory improvers codesign change ideas, leveraging the collective wisdom and expertise of all stakeholders, to address the unique needs and aspirations of their educational communities. Through collaboration, they forge alliances, build capacity, and cultivate a sense of ownership and commitment to equitable outcomes. Liberatory improvers understand the necessity of sharing power as a significant part of their collaborative efforts and work to disrupt hierarchies, biases, and systems of domination, while centering the voices, agency, and self-determination of those who have historically been marginalized. We explore the role of power and discuss power sharing in Chapter 6. Recognizing the need for marginalized folks to be agents of their own liberation, liberatory improvers regularly empower students, authentically engaging them as strategists and tacticians in the improvement processes.

4. Culturally Sustaining Pedagogy. Liberatory improvers deeply value and embrace culturally sustaining pedagogy as a core disposition in their work. This pedagogical approach recognizes and honors the diverse cultural and linguistic assets that students bring to the learning environment. Liberatory improvers are committed to affirming and celebrating the identities, languages, and cultural backgrounds of all learners. These leaders understand that meaningful learning occurs when students' lived experiences are bridged with academic content. They prioritize instructional practices that establish connections between the curriculum and students' cultural knowledge and perspectives. By doing so, they create a learning environment that is relevant, engaging, and meaningful for every student.

A key aspect of this disposition is countering deficit-based narratives and challenging stereotypes. They reject the notion that students from marginalized backgrounds are lacking or are deficient in some way, and they find opportunities to uplift counternarratives that dispel these myths. Additionally, liberatory improvers intentionally provide culturally relevant and responsive teaching that recognizes and builds on the strengths and assets of students. By doing this, they foster a sense of belonging, respect, and empowerment among learners.

Inclusive learning environments are at the heart of liberatory improvers' practice. They actively work to create classrooms where students' cultural identities are valued and honored. Liberatory improvers promote cultural pride by incorporating diverse perspectives and experiences into the curriculum. They encourage students to explore their own cultural backgrounds while fostering a deep appreciation for the diversity of their peers. Additionally, they foster reciprocal relationships between students and educators, where mutual respect and understanding are central. Through embracing culturally sustaining pedagogy, liberatory improvers create classrooms that not only support academic achievement but also facilitate the development of students' identities and critical consciousness. Students are encouraged to explore and understand their own cultural heritage and the experiences of others. This approach cultivates a deep sense of self-worth, empowerment, and social awareness.

5. Intersectional and Asset-Based Approaches. Intersectional and asset-based approaches are fundamental dispositions of liberatory improvers. These leaders recognize the intersecting dimensions of students' identities and the systemic inequities that arise from the intersections of race, gender, class, and other social identities. Liberatory improvers adopt an intersectional lens that acknowledges the complex ways in which students experience privilege and oppression simultaneously and develop new methods for assessing the climate and culture of their school or district that decentralize the experiences of dominant identity groups and privilege the realities of those on the margins. In Chapter 2, we discussed how centering the experiences of marginalized and multi-marginalized students and capturing the stories of socially homeless students provides a more nuanced understanding of the climate and culture of the school or district. That approach is the enactment of this disposition.

For liberatory improvers, schools serve as places that foster not only academic endeavors but also the cultivation of activists working toward the democratic rebuilding of our society (Marshall & Oliva, 2006). They see all students as potential agents of change and understand that students possess diverse strengths, talents, and lived experiences, which are valuable assets for their learning and development. They view their students through an appreciative inquiry lens, intentionally focusing on strengths, possibilities, and positive experiences, rather than on problems and deficiencies. (Note: We delve further into appreciative inquiry in Chapter 4.) By embracing an asset-based approach, liberatory improvers challenge deficit-based narratives and honor the inherent potential of all students. They intentionally design inclusive policies, practices, and interventions that celebrate and build on students' assets, fostering empowerment, resilience, and holistic growth.

6. Ethical Leadership and Sustainable Change. Ethical leadership and sustainable change are core dispositions of liberatory improvers. First, these leaders are deeply committed to upholding high ethical standards in their leadership practices. They understand the importance of integrity, transparency, and social justice. They believe that their decisions and actions should always prioritize the well-being and rights of marginalized individuals and communities. It's not just about doing what's convenient or beneficial for themselves; it's about making choices that align with their ethical principles and contribute to a more equitable and inclusive society. One distinctive characteristic of liberatory improvers is their openness to questions and critical inquiry. They welcome others to ask them about their thinking process or the reasoning behind their decisions. Why? Because they see it as an opportunity to give others a sneak peek into their ethics. By being transparent and explaining the rationale behind their choices, they aim to foster understanding and trust. They want others to see that their decisions are not arbitrary or self-serving, but rather grounded in a thoughtful and principled approach. They invite people to engage in meaningful dialogue and hold them accountable for their actions.

Liberatory improvers navigate complex ethical dilemmas, ensuring that their actions prioritize equity and avoid perpetuating harm. They advocate for systemic shifts that promote long-term equitable outcomes, seeking to dismantle oppressive systems and structures while working toward sustainable change. These leaders recognize that achieving equity requires ongoing dedication, perseverance, and collaboration, and they actively promote the sustainability of change efforts by cultivating shared leadership, building capacity, and fostering a culture of continuous improvement. Liberatory improvers see equity issues as adaptive challenges and find comfort in iterative processes that align with their relentless pursuit of social justice. They understand that this iterative process has the potential to change people's values, beliefs, roles, relationships, and approaches to how to accomplish equity-focused goals.

7. Transformative Relationships. The next disposition that sets liberatory improvers apart is their emphasis on transformative relationships. They view improvement work as a deeply human endeavor, which means they recognize the inherent goodness in others and actively strive to cultivate relationships that go beyond mere transactions. For liberatory improvers, transformative relationships are not solely about changing or influencing others. They understand that these relationships offer opportunities for personal growth and expansion for themselves as well. It's a two-way street. They approach relationships with care, compassion, vulnerability, curiosity, and love. These qualities foster an environment where individuals can exchange pieces of their humanity with one another.

When it comes to relationships, liberatory improvers are unapologetic in their focus on compassion and care for others. They actively work to create empathetic holding environments. These environments provide crucial support for individuals as they navigate the challenges and disequilibrium that often accompany the process of change. By extending care and understanding, liberatory improvers build deep trust within these relationships. In fact, this deep sense of trust has a profound impact on the collective self-efficacy of the organization or community. Liberatory improvers recognize that failure is a natural part of the improvement process, and they normalize it. They create spaces where it's safe to make mistakes and learn from them. They embrace the iterative and experimental nature of improvement, understanding that it takes time and a willingness to adapt.

8. Constructivist Mindset. Finally, liberatory improvers embrace a constructivist mindset, which fundamentally shapes their approach to understanding the world and driving change. This mindset is rooted in the belief that meaning and truth are not fixed or objective entities waiting to be discovered. Instead, they are actively cocreated through transformative relationships and shared experiences. For liberatory improvers, knowledge and understanding are not imposed from above or held exclusively by a select few. They recognize that everyone possesses unique perspectives, insights, and knowledge that contribute to the construction of meaning. This understanding fosters a deep sense of respect for diverse viewpoints and encourages active dialogue and collaboration. Because of their constructivist mindset, liberatory improvers view knowledge as a dynamic and evolving process. They understand that different contexts, cultures, and historical factors shape people's understanding of the world. Consequently, they approach improvement work with a humility that acknowledges their own limitations and the need to constantly learn and adapt.

This constructivist mindset enables liberatory improvers to challenge dominant narratives and dismantle traditional power structures. They recognize that these narratives often reflect the perspectives of the privileged and may perpetuate inequities. By embracing diverse perspectives and cocreating meaning, they seek to dismantle oppressive systems and foster inclusive, equitable environments. Furthermore, this constructivist mindset emphasizes the importance of experiential learning. Liberatory improvers understand that knowledge and understanding are not solely obtained through passive consumption of information but through active engagement, reflection, and dialogue. They encourage individuals to critically analyze their experiences, question assumptions, and challenge existing paradigms.

AT YOUR DESK OR IN THE HALLS

Liberatory improvement challenges the status quo and invites educators to engage in a continuous journey of self-reflection, growth, and action. By embodying the dispositions of liberatory improvers, educators can become catalysts for transformative change, dismantling oppressive systems and creating inclusive and empowering educational environments. But we know that every catalyst is only as effective as the change tools available. We see improvement science as a useful set of tools for liberatory improvers focused on taking a systematic approach to identifying and addressing educational inequities because its data-driven and iterative nature aligns well with the goal of advancing equity. Further, we believe the use of these tools promotes the reflection, refinement, and adaptation of improvement strategies and fosters a culture where individual educators continuously examine their practices, challenge assumptions, and refine their strategies to better meet the needs of marginalized students.

Throughout this chapter, we have explored the dispositions necessary for educators to engage in liberatory improvement, the specific practices that bridge equity and improvement science, and the integration of improvement science and equity-focused dispositions. By embodying these dispositions and utilizing improvement science tools and processes, liberatory improvers can create a powerful synergy that advances equity, social justice, and improved outcomes for marginalized students. It is through the intentional cultivation of these dispositions that educators can embody the essence of liberatory improvers.

Through this integration, we can pave the way for a future where all students, regardless of their background, have equitable opportunities to thrive, succeed, and realize their full potential. It is through the collective efforts of educators, researchers, policymakers, and advocates that we can transform education into a liberatory space where every student's unique identity is valued, celebrated, and empowered.

Reflection Questions

- Do I identify with the idea of being a liberatory improver? Why or why not?
- Which of the liberatory improvement dispositions am I most confident that I possess, and which do I want to develop?
- How might I go about cultivating these dispositions in others?
- How do these dispositions show up in the workings of my school or district?

CHAPTER 4

The Adjacent Possible

Some science fiction seems impossibly far removed from what might ever happen, and some describes what seems within the realms of possibility based on the world we already know. *Star Trek* is a great example of both. While we don't profess to have any significant expertise on *Star Trek*, the show can serve as a lens for how we think about the future. Because if equity is the vision, then we have too few examples of what that actually looks like in practice. And as we will see in this chapter and the next, if educators are expected to work toward a desired outcome (whether that involves equity), then believing that they are being asked to achieve something that is in fact within reach is important.

Star Trek is a science fiction television series and franchise that explores a future where humans have advanced technologically and socially to the point of being able to travel through space and interact with extraterrestrial civilizations. Although the series is famous for implausible ideas like warp speed and traveling to other galaxies, it is an exploration of the adjacent possible—a future that is not entirely disconnected from our present reality—and builds on it by exploring new technologies, social structures, and scientific advancements that are plausibly within reach. We believe that it's important to focus on the adjacent possible, especially when talking about equity, because for so many educators, their experience with "doing equity" is of having to digest uncomfortable truths about how inequitable the current system is.

The Reverend Dr. Martin Luther King Jr. was a fan, and he urged Nichelle Nichols, the Black actress who played Uhura as part of a multiracial bridge crew, to stay on the show when she was thinking of leaving, precisely because he knew that her presence helped Americans form a mental picture of what a world without segregation might look like. In the context of racial representation on television in the 1960s, the adjacent possible was limited. Opportunities for Black actors, especially in leading and nonstereotypical roles, were scarce. However, the existence of *Star Trek* and the character of Uhura created a small opening—a door that was cracked open toward greater inclusivity and diversity. Dr. King recognized this opportunity and understood the potential impact that Nichols's portrayal of Uhura could have on breaking racial barriers. By encouraging her to stay in her role, he was advocating for the exploration of the adjacent possible. He believed that by persisting and being a positive role model, Nichols could contribute to expanding the realm of possibilities for racial representation in the entertainment industry.

The adjacent possible, a term first used by biologist Stuart Kauffman, is the space between reality and fantasy. It hasn't happened yet, but it appears to be within reach. It is both desirable and feasible. In the case of *Star Trek*, the show's writers and creators drew on the scientific and technological knowledge of their time and imagined a future that builds on that knowledge. In addition to technical advances, *Star Trek*'s vision of the future also involves social and political improvements that are within reach of our current society; the show's portrayal of a society without poverty or discrimination, where people work together toward a common goal of exploration and discovery, is an extension of our current aspirations toward social justice and equality. While the technological aspect of *Star Trek* builds on the future possibilities of scientific research, the societal aspect of the show evinces the writers' and creators' beliefs about people. Although they had little experience living in a world without poverty or discrimination, they believed people are capable of collaborating and cocreating a more just society. In their creation of a future world that fits within the neighborhood of our current reality, *Star Trek*'s creative team painted a picture of how technological and social change can evolve.

As leaders, we are expected to develop a vision for the future and identify strategies to achieve it. Almost all schools and districts have vision statements, and increasingly these are in the form of a "vision of the graduate." Additionally, those statements almost always include the words "all students," and so they are, in a narrow and technical sense, about equity. But they frequently represent a kind of "soft" equity (Welton et al., 2018), one that does not put too much strain on current conditions or challenge traditions. We are not suggesting that vision statements should not include the word "all"; rather, that the development of a goal of any size (vision/goal/objective/aim) should be accompanied by a conversation about the connotation of words when it is accepted that there is no such thing as equity-neutral and that all plans, from 5-year strategic plans to plan-do-study-act (PDSA) cycles, must be explicitly engineered toward meeting an equity-focused goal.

Our ability to imagine the adjacent possible is directly tied to our understanding of the current apparatus and what we think people are capable of. In our work with school and district leaders, we have found general agreement on the need to stay abreast of educational research. Leaders often look to scholars to assist in the identification of research- and evidence-based practices designed to make progress toward outcome goals. While focusing on the possibilities of technological change is a typical component of leadership, surfacing our beliefs about what we think people are capable of is not.

Our beliefs about what people are capable of can shape the boundaries of the adjacent possible, influencing what we perceive as possible or impossible and what we are willing to explore and pursue. For example, if we believe that humans are capable of achieving great feats of technological and social progress, we may be more inclined to explore and pursue new ideas and possibilities that push the boundaries of what is currently known or knowable. Conversely, if we hold limiting beliefs about what people are capable of, such as believing that certain groups or individuals are inherently inferior or unable to achieve certain goals, we may be more likely to dismiss or overlook potential innovations and possibilities that fall outside of our preconceived notions of what is possible. Consider the deficit ideology about students from low-income families. Many educators, consciously or not, believe that low-income students are less capable of academic success. As a result, these students are often placed in lower-level classes and receive less support. When this type of thinking is pervasive, changing outcomes requires challenging these limiting beliefs.

Beliefs about what people are capable of can also influence the types of collaborations and partnerships that are formed to explore the adjacent possible. If we believe that innovation and progress are the exclusive domain of a select few, we may be less likely to collaborate and share resources with others who come from different backgrounds or disciplines. On the other hand, if we believe that innovation and progress are collective and collaborative endeavors, we may be more likely to seek out diverse perspectives and collaborate with others who have different skills and knowledge, opening up new possibilities for exploration and development.

LIMITATIONS OF TRADITIONAL MENTAL MODELS

As authors, we hope that you were nodding along as you've been reading this chapter or vigorously highlighting all of the ideas about the adjacent possible that you agreed with. If that is the case, your response is very similar to the educators we've supported in their improvement efforts. Given the widespread support for taking an adjacent possible approach to imagining the future, why hasn't it become a part of our standard practice as educators? We believe traditional mental models of visionary leadership, data-driven decision-making, and an overreliance on developing specific, measurable, achievable, relevant, and time-bound (SMART) goals have hindered our ability to cast a liberatory vision for the future. Additionally, we believe the normalization of deficit thinking within the field of education diminishes our capacity to envision a future that is more than merely a slightly better version of the status quo.

Visionary Leadership. Visionary leadership has long been held as a hallmark of effective leadership in education. It places significant emphasis on a single leader's vision and often neglects the voices and perspectives of other stakeholders. Despite the research that highlights the importance of developing a shared vision that is rooted and grounded in the lived experiences of all stakeholders and represents the values and beliefs of the collective, we, as a profession, are often smitten by charismatic leaders who develop plans for the future in isolation. But why? Tema Okun's (2021) framework, White supremacy culture (WSC), provides valuable insights into how this mental model reinforces oppressive systems and undermines collaborative efforts.

Within the context of visionary leadership, power tends to be concentrated in the hands of a single leader or a small group, reinforcing hierarchical structures. This concentration of power can inhibit the active participation of stakeholders, including students, in decision-making processes and the co-construction of visions. According to Okun, power hoarding (which we discuss further in Chapter 6) is a characteristic of WSC, where power and decision-making authority are concentrated in the hands of a few. This approach limits the diversity of perspectives and voices that influence educational practices, perpetuating systemic inequities. Traditional mental models of visionary leadership often prioritize the ideas and visions of a single leader over collective imagination and collaboration. This emphasis on individualism can hinder the development of inclusive and equitable educational environments.

Okun identifies individualism as another aspect of WSC. It values personal achievement, competition, and independence over collective efforts. This focus on individual success may undermine the collaborative processes needed for co-constructing visions that address the unique needs and experiences of all stakeholders, particularly marginalized communities. By prioritizing power hoarding and individualism, traditional visionary leadership mental models perpetuate systems of privilege and reinforce the marginalization of certain groups. This approach is incongruent with the liberatory approach's fundamental principles, which emphasize collective imagination, shared power, and the dismantling of oppressive structures.

Data-Driven Decision-Making. In the realm of educational leadership, data-driven decision-making has gained significant prominence over the years. This approach, often associated with accountability models such as No Child Left Behind and other standardized testing initiatives, has placed a heavy emphasis on quantitative data as the primary driver for decision-making. While data can provide valuable insights, the overemphasis on traditional mental models can stifle our ability to envision the adjacent possible and limit our progress toward equity and justice.

The traditional model of data-driven decision-making places excessive weight on numerical outcome measures, such as test scores and graduation rates, to measure educational success. While these indicators offer a snapshot of student performance, they fail to capture the complex, multifaceted nature of learning and the broader societal factors that influence educational outcomes—especially those related to equity. Relying solely on quantitative data neglects the rich context of students' lived experiences, backgrounds, and the systemic inequities they face. Moreover, the narrow focus on quantitative data perpetuates a deficit-oriented perspective, often reinforcing existing inequities rather than addressing their root causes. It places disproportionate blame on individual students and teachers, overshadowing the systemic barriers and societal factors that contribute to disparities in educational outcomes. This limited view obstructs the envisioning of a more just and equitable future, as it fails to challenge the underlying structures and policies that sustain inequality. As a result, it is easy to fall into the trap of constructing a vision for the future that is solely focused on improved scores on quantitative metrics.

If we are to explore the possibilities of creating a more equitable future for students, we must break free from the confines of traditional data-driven decision-making and foster a liberatory approach. Safir's (2017) concept of "street data" provides a useful frame for dismantling traditional mental models about how we use data. Street data refers to the firsthand experiences, stories, and qualitative observations gathered from students, educators, families, and community members. It recognizes the importance of diverse perspectives and lived experiences, grounding decision-making in the reality of the educational context.

By incorporating street data into the visioning phase of educational improvement, leaders can gain a more comprehensive understanding of the complex factors influencing student learning and success. Street data captures the nuances and cultural context that quantitative data alone cannot, allowing for a more holistic and nuanced approach to envisioning and implementing equitable practices. Furthermore, street data enable educational leaders to center the voices of marginalized communities and amplify their experiences. By valuing these narratives, leaders can challenge the dominant narratives perpetuated by quantitative data, disrupting the power dynamics that marginalize certain groups and limiting progress toward justice and equity. Incorporating street data during the visioning phase empowers stakeholders, including students, to co-construct a more inclusive and transformative vision for their educational environment. It promotes dialogue, collaboration, and shared ownership, breaking away from the top-down decision-making processes that often exclude marginalized voices.

SMART Goals. What kind of goals did we have before they were SMART? Or maybe a better question is: "If developing SMART goals is the answer, what is the question?" SMART goals have been widely adopted in educational settings as a means of setting targets and measuring progress. While SMART goals provide a structured framework, they often prioritize short-term outcomes and fail to capture the transformative and systemic change necessary to address educational inequities.

Not only do we expect every goal to be SMART, but over time we have come to believe that if a goal or objective is not SMART, it must not be worth pursuing. Our focus on developing and obtaining SMART goals has caused us to overfocus on goals that can be measured using quantitative data while ignoring the importance of experience, processes, and progress. While we are not suggesting that goals should not be SMART, we recognize the impact this focus has on how we approach improvements across all areas.

The concept of SMART goals was first introduced by George T. Doran (1981), a consultant and former director of corporate planning for Washington Water Power Company. While the concept was initially developed for use in the business world, it was soon adapted for use in education and other fields. Many educators believe that effective goals and objectives must incorporate all five elements of SMART; we have certainly sat through our fair share of school improvement planning workshops during which the presenter made that case. Doran himself explained that the acronym doesn't mean that every objective written will have all five criteria. Unfortunately, in education we have used the SMART format as a requirement rather than a heuristic, which has led to compliance rather than strategic thinking.

Not only do goals not need to be SMART, they also don't need to be quantitative, nor do they need to be outcome-based. Depending on how challenging the goal, it may take a long time to reach, and progress toward the goal may not be a straight, upward slope (Fullan, 2007). Setting people outcome goals that they do not know how to reach may actually interfere with progress toward the goal, as people tend to cycle quickly through approaches that they think might lead to a quick fix, rather than methodically analyzing the problem, generating several possible courses of action, and running experiments based on their best hypothesis for what will create the best results. In other words, outcome-focused goals may interfere with learning (Seijts et al., 2004).

Goals and the adjacent possible can leverage each other. For example, understanding the adjacent possible can inform the development of goals by helping individuals and organizations identify the most promising and realistic goals based on their current knowledge and resources. Similarly, using goals can help individuals and organizations explore the adjacent possible by setting clear objectives and tracking their progress toward achieving them. This liberatory approach challenges the narrow focus of goals and encourages educational leaders to explore broader possibilities. It invites leaders to engage in a critical examination of the existing systems, structures, and practices that perpetuate inequities. By embracing a liberatory approach, leaders can envision transformative goals that foster authentic student engagement, social justice, and sustainable change.

LEVERAGING THE ADJACENT POSSIBLE

The adjacent possible helps to flip the script: Instead of focusing on barriers, limitations, constraints, and other reasons why the status quo is hard to change, it changes the conversation to one that is more inspiring and challenges educators to design steps to create a new reality rather than bemoaning the state of the current one. Deficit thinking is rooted in a focus on problems, deficiencies, and what is not working in an organization or system. In the worst case, the deficits in question are attributed to already marginalized students rather than the system that creates those deficits, reinforcing negative stereotypes and perpetuating inequity. To truly transform our educational landscapes, we must adopt a liberatory approach—one that embraces the adjacent possible, illuminates the power of positive deviants and bright spots, and fosters a mindset of abundance and possibility. Several fields of inquiry allow entry into a much more generative space; here we describe some well-developed ways of entering into the adjacent possible.

Positive Deviance. Defying the gravity of deficit thinking, educators can elevate their practice by deliberately shifting their focus toward positive deviants—the individuals and organizations that demonstrate exceptional outcomes or practices with the same, or sometimes fewer, resources as their peers. By studying these outliers, educators gain valuable insights into the factors and strategies that contribute to success. This empowers them to challenge the status quo and reimagine what is possible within their own contexts.

The significance of positive deviants was documented in Vietnam in the 1970s, when Jerry Sternin worked with mothers whose children were not suffering from the same ailments caused by malnutrition as their peers to codify and replicate their practices, thereby improving the health of large numbers of children (Pascale et al., 2010). But we have other more recent and just as compelling examples to learn from. In the weeks immediately following the release of the COVID-19 vaccine, people living in Chicago's northern, affluent suburbs were much more likely to have been vaccinated than people living in the city itself, and less than 40% of the vaccinations administered in Chicago were given to people living in high- or medium-risk neighborhoods—neighborhoods that had been hardest hit by COVID-19 and whose residents were primarily Black and Hispanic (St. Clair et al., 2021). As quoted in the *Chicago Tribune*, an elected official from one of the poorer neighborhoods said, "This is not a surprise to anyone in the Black community because this is the norm. And it won't be easily fixed until we give Black and brown communities the same access to health care and a healthy lifestyle as we do people on the North Side and the suburbs."

But as the article goes on to explain, some medical providers were far more successful than others at delivering vaccinations to those living in poorer parts of the city. The initial target was to vaccinate as many people as possible, but that practice favored those with access to computers and good Wi-Fi, the time to sit at a computer hitting refresh, and the time and transportation to travel what could have been significant distances to a facility that could offer them the vaccine. A goal focused on a number quickly led to inequity—a point that comes up throughout this book. But even when the goal shifted to prioritizing hardest-hit ZIP codes, not all providers had relationships with the people who needed the vaccine, many of whom did not have a primary care provider. So the providers who anticipated the issues with reaching the most-at risk city residents hired local residents to conduct house-to-house outreach, speaking to residents in their native language and calling the hospital on their request to make appointments for them—in other words, reducing the friction that was a large part of trying to access the vaccine early in the process.

These innovations, along with many others, were the practices that made some medical organizations more successful than others, despite the fact that they were not the largest or the best resourced. Positive deviants, or "bright spots" (Heath & Heath, 2011), represent beacons of hope within our educational systems, where success and achievement shine even in the face of adversity. When we shine a light on these exceptional examples, we uncover a rich tapestry of innovative strategies, pedagogical approaches, and supportive structures that can be shared and scaled to benefit all learners. By immersing ourselves in the stories of positive deviants, we embark on a journey of possibility. We come face-to-face with educators who, against the odds, have discovered transformative practices to unlock the full potential of their students. Their experiences challenge the prevailing narratives of what is achievable, opening up a world of opportunities for those who are willing to embrace change and strive for improvement. But just as importantly, studying what they have done can lead to the creation of a roadmap that allows others to replicate their success.

When we talk about the power of positive deviants, we often hear from educators who understand the importance of leveraging bright spots but struggle to find specific bright spots when it comes to issues of equity. This should come as no surprise given the structural nature of -isms we fight against. But focusing on bright spots encourages us to look for successful practices in unexpected places. What do we know about places where the results are better than others? When faced with addressing disproportionate outcomes, we have traditionally focused our investigative work on trying to figure out why things aren't working for students of color. But how would our work look different if we started by asking ourselves why things are working for White students?

This more nuanced question leads us to look beyond the surface of instructional delivery and explore other factors like belonging. As Geoffrey Cohen (2022) points out, "Students who report a strong sense of belonging tend to be more motivated to learn, perform better academically, have better rates of attendance, engage in less misconduct and fewer health-threatening behaviors, and have higher self-esteem and a better mental health" (p. 213). If a sense of belonging is a prerequisite for learning, then it behooves equity-focused improvers to unearth how educators create belonging environments for students who are already meeting or exceeding expected outcomes. This subtle shift can push our future thinking from a better version of the status quo (e.g., improved test scores for students of color) to the adjacent possible (e.g., improved learning conditions for students of color) that represents the uncharted territories of learning and achievement that lie within our grasp if we dare to venture beyond the boundaries of tradition and mediocrity.

One note of caution. It's important to ask educators to identify the positive deviants in their schools and districts after doing the work of creating an equity-focused vision for the adjacent possible—and after having a conversation about how you would define a positive deviant. Just as there is no such thing as an equity-neutral strategy or practice, there is no such thing as an equity-neutral positive deviant. We suggest that educators identifying positive deviants pay more attention to growth scores than achievement scores; disaggregate data by race, gender, and ability; and triangulate data by interviewing students about teachers who have high growth scores, because they are always very insightful. In fact, students are frequently more astute about good instruction than the supervisors of their teachers. We have been in more than one conversation when the interviews with students revealed an extraordinary amount of detail about the practices of the outstanding teachers in a school—detail that could then be used to construct a pathway for other teachers to follow, which in improvement science is known as a change package.

One of the key principles of positive deviance is the belief that solutions are already present within the system—this is a tradition that goes back to the work of Kurt Lewin (1946) in the years after the Second World War. As an educational leader, your role is to facilitate a process of exploration and discovery, empowering your teachers, staff, and students to identify and share the innovative practices that have led to exceptional outcomes. This process requires creating a supportive and collaborative environment, fostering trust, and encouraging open communication. By valuing the diverse perspectives and experiences within your educational community, you can tap into a wealth of knowledge and harness the collective wisdom of your stakeholders.

Positive deviance challenges the notion that all problems require external solutions. Instead, it urges you to look inward and recognize that the potential for positive change lies within your schools and district. By embracing a strengths-based approach and focusing on what is working well, you can inspire a culture of continuous improvement and innovation. Celebrating and amplifying the positive deviant behaviors within your educational community creates a ripple effect, inspiring others to think outside the box, take calculated risks, and challenge the status quo.

Appreciative Inquiry. Appreciative inquiry (AI) is a philosophical and methodological approach to organizational and personal development that emphasizes the power of positive questions and conversations. It is based on the belief that organizations and individuals tend to move in the direction of their inquiries and conversations. In other words, what we focus on and ask about shapes our thinking, actions, and ultimately, our outcomes. It was developed at Case Western Reserve University in the 1980s and has gained recognition as a valuable tool for organizational development and change management (Cooperrider et al., 2008).

The central idea behind AI is that by intentionally focusing on strengths, possibilities, and positive experiences rather than problems and deficiencies, we can catalyze positive change and growth. AI encourages individuals and organizations to identify and build on their existing assets, resources, and successes. This positive framing fosters a sense of empowerment, motivation, and collective ownership among participants. Traditional leadership models often focus on identifying problems and implementing strategies to fix them. However, AI shifts the focus to identifying and amplifying strengths and successes within the educational community.

For example, let's say a school district is facing significant achievement gaps between students of different socioeconomic backgrounds. The traditional approach might involve focusing on the deficiencies and problems within the underperforming groups, asking questions like, "What are the barriers preventing these students from succeeding?" or "What are the deficits in their academic preparation?" This deficit-based approach can lead to a narrative that reinforces stereotypes and perpetuates a sense of hopelessness. It may result in remedial interventions and deficit-oriented policies that view these students as lacking and needing to be "fixed." However, by applying the principles of AI, the district shifts its focus to strengths and possibilities. Sometimes, improving outcomes begins with asking the right questions like, "What are the success stories of students from similar backgrounds who have overcome challenges?" or "What are the strategies employed by teachers who have achieved positive outcomes with these students?"

This shift in focus opens up a space for identifying and amplifying existing assets and successful practices. The district may discover that some teachers have developed culturally responsive instructional approaches that engage and empower students from diverse backgrounds. They may find examples of supportive mentoring programs or community partnerships that have positively impacted student achievement. By sharing these success stories and uplifting best practices, the district starts to shape a new narrative and collective mindset. Teachers and administrators begin to see these students not as deficient, but as capable and full of potential. The conversations and inquiries around strengths and possibilities lead to a change in thinking and a new set of actions.

In our improvement work with districts, we highlight the utility of an asset-based approach when analyzing data that deviates from the expected norm. Traditional data analysis focuses on negative deviants. In improvement science, negative deviants are individuals or groups whose behaviors or outcomes are worse than the norm. They are often studied to understand what factors contribute to their poor performance and to identify ways to improve the overall system or community. Positive deviants, on the other hand, as mentioned previously, are individuals or groups whose behaviors or outcomes are better than the norm. They are studied to identify the strategies or practices that they use to achieve exceptional results, with the goal of spreading these practices to others in the system or community to improve overall outcomes. Negative deviant stories are designed to help us understand what needs to change, and positive deviant stories, or bright spots, help us identify change ideas that can lead to improved outcomes.

Storytelling. Throughout this book, we cite storytelling as a valuable tool in improvement science, as it allows for the sharing of experiences and perspectives in a way that can help identify and address problems more effectively and engagingly. Stories can help highlight areas in which improvement is needed by providing insight into the experiences of those affected by a particular process or system. By listening to the stories of stakeholders, improvement teams can gain a better understanding of the challenges they face and identify opportunities for change. Storytelling can be used to engage stakeholders in the improvement process by providing a platform for them to share their experiences and perspectives. By giving stakeholders a voice in the process, improvement teams can build trust and foster a sense of ownership and commitment to the improvement effort. Stories can be used to communicate the progress of improvement efforts and highlight the impact of change. Improvement teams can build momentum and inspire others to join the effort by sharing stories of success. Within the context of exploring the adjacent possible, stories help us consider ways we can build on current technologies that have been successful and illuminate what people are capable of. Often the stories that encourage us to reconsider the possibilities of the future are crafted to challenge the dominant narratives that limit possibilities. Although this approach to telling counternarratives to spark the considerations for the future exists in many settings, it is baked into the traditions of historically Black churches, particularly testimony service, so that is the example that we lean on here.

Historically, testimony service has been a central part of many Black church services, providing an opportunity for members to express their gratitude, share their struggles and challenges, and give testimony to the power of God in their lives. During testimony service, individuals come to the front of the church or stand up in their seats to share their stories. They may speak about their personal experiences with illness, loss, family, work, and relationships. They may also express gratitude for blessings and the goodness of God in their lives. The format and length of testimony services may vary depending on the church, but they are often spontaneous and heartfelt. Testimony service is seen as an important part of Black church culture, as it allows individuals to connect, build community, and inspire each other through personal stories. They are also seen as a way to honor the African oral tradition, in which stories are used to pass down knowledge, wisdom, and values from one generation to the next.

Research on storytelling in the Black church suggests that the use of testimony service can help individuals imagine a more just and equitable future. In her study on the role of testimony service in the Black church, Lowe (2012) emphasizes that storytelling through testimonies helps African American congregations develop a collective memory of resilience and survival. Testimonies enable individuals to share personal experiences, confront challenges, and inspire others, fostering a sense of hope and perseverance within the community. Another study by Koenig et al. (2018) examined the impact of a testimony-based intervention on mental health outcomes among Black adults. The researchers found that participants in the intervention group reported greater improvements in mental health and spiritual well-being compared to those in the control group. The intervention involved sharing personal stories of struggles and triumphs in small groups, which allowed participants to build supportive relationships and foster a sense of community.

So, what makes testimony service and/or the use of counternarratives such a powerful tool in imagining the adjacent possible? During their testimony, an individual usually recounts an event, typically negative, and talks about how God intervened to produce a positive outcome. Although there are no specific criteria to determine what makes a "good" testimony (real life is not composed of rubrics), congregants often respond more enthusiastically to testimonies that highlight negative events or challenges that are common to other congregants. Within the Black church, testimonies often tap into people's shared experiences with racism, financial oppression, and/or lack of opportunities. As we consider storytelling as a tool for exploring the adjacent possible, we should consider lessons learned from testimony service:

- Testimonies are local stories told by local people about shared local problems. They rely on familiarity and shared experiences. It's the ubiquitous nature of the problems that holds such great power and can shift mindsets. When folks encounter the same obstacle that was testified about on Sunday, they are better positioned to see the issue through new eyes and envision a different outcome based on the testifier's experience.

- Although it is okay to share someone else's story, the best testimonies are personalized and provide the speaker with a space in which their lived experience is centered. Testimonies challenge dominant narratives by allowing individuals who typically sit silently on the margins to share their personal stories and perspectives. Traditionally, testimony service was the time to highlight counternarratives that both legitimize the lived experiences of folks on the margins and build personal and collective self-efficacy. In this sense, the testimony service acts as a liberatory space in which the testifier and the congregation can feel seen, heard, and valued.

- Testimonies are initiated by "ordinary" people who attribute their extraordinary or unanticipated positive outcomes to their relationship with God and their connection to the congregation. Testimonies are not stories about heroes whose successful outcomes are the result of their acts. Instead, they are a reminder that ordinary folks are capable of extraordinary things when they eschew the individualistic nature of our society and embrace a relational approach to life that privileges the collective wisdom of the congregation.

- The best testimonies dig into the details of the process that led to the outcome. A typical testimony spends little time explaining the problem; there is no need to when discussing common challenges that plague most congregants. Instead, they focus on the process—how did I approach the issue differently this time? Rooted in the understanding that you have to do what you never did to get what you never had, great testimonies gift the congregants with change ideas or simple steps they can take to change their outcomes.

- Testimonies build a sense of community and solidarity among members because they require vulnerability from the speaker and empathetic listening from the congregation. Testimonies often involve overcoming challenges and adversity, which can inspire and empower others facing similar struggles. By sharing stories of resilience, congregants find strength in their vulnerabilities and help others find strength in theirs. This shared resilience creates a sense of community, support, and encouragement among members who are navigating similar journeys.

- Testimony services decenter power, rationality, and authority. While there are no explicit rules about who is allowed to speak, there is a general understanding that the testimony service is not for the preacher. Although the service is often kicked off by someone with a title (e.g., deacon) who models a good testimony, it is an opportunity to hear from regular folks who are working daily to live out their Christian beliefs.

- The best testimonies are honest about successes and failures and highlight the individual's shift from traditional thinking to God's thinking, which pushes them beyond what they previously believed they were capable of. Testimonies are not seen as opportunities to tell self-aggrandizing stories. They invite individuals to connect through shared experiences, challenges, and failures. They promote a sense of collective identity by highlighting the ways we can learn from others' missteps and mistakes. By recognizing their shared struggles, individuals within a community can come together to support one another, leading to a stronger sense of solidarity.

- Testimonies help people reconsider what they are capable of as individuals (self-efficacy) and what they can accomplish as a group (collective self-efficacy). When people see their own stories represented and validated, they can develop a sense of empowerment and realize that their voices matter. This recognition enhances personal self-efficacy by instilling the belief that individuals have the capacity to make a difference and affect change. By presenting alternative perspectives and offering nuanced interpretations of events, testimonies provide a fresh lens through which individuals can critically analyze existing power structures and biases. This critical engagement fosters a sense of collective self-efficacy by demonstrating that change is possible and that collective action can challenge and transform societal norms.

AT YOUR DESK OR IN THE HALLS

The concept of the adjacent possible suggests that the future is not prede-termined but emerges through the exploration of possibilities adjacent to the current state. In the context of educational leadership, co-constructing the adjacent possible involves engaging stakeholders, including students, in imagining and creating possibilities that go beyond existing mental models. We know from experience that when students are actively involved in shaping their educational experiences, they gain a sense of ownership and agency. By including students in the co-construction of the adjacent possible, educational leaders not only empower them but also tap into their unique insights, experiences, and aspirations. Students are more likely to feel valued and heard, which fosters a positive school climate and strengthens their commitment to learning.

By creating spaces for dialogue, collaboration, and collective dreaming, educational leaders can tap into the diverse perspectives and knowledge within their communities. This process fosters ownership, empowerment, and a sense of agency among stakeholders, ultimately leading to more equitable and just educational practices. In addition to serving as a tool to improve our ability to unearth our equitable aspirations and imagine a more just future, exploring the adjacent possible is a liberatory approach. The adjacent possible refers to the realm of possibilities that are attainable from the existing conditions and resources available to us.

As educational leaders, we have a responsibility to create a future that truly meets the needs of all students. To achieve this goal, we must embrace a liberatory approach when crafting a vision for the future that engages all stakeholders in co-constructing the adjacent possible. By focusing on storytelling, identifying and learning from bright spots, and working to build self-efficacy, this approach can break traditional mental models of visionary leadership, data-driven decision-making, and an overreliance on developing SMART goals. These models often prioritize efficiency and standardization over equity and justice. Further, they can lead to a narrow focus on test scores and other quantitative measures of success, rather than on the holistic needs of students. They can also perpetuate systemic inequities by failing to address the root causes of educational disparities.

To overcome these limitations, we must embrace a more nuanced process for developing a vision for the future that is grounded in a liberatory approach to improvement science. This approach requires us to engage all stakeholders in co-constructing the adjacent possible through storytelling and building self-efficacy. By doing so, we can create a more just and equitable educational landscape that meets the needs of all students. If we are to put these ideas into practice, we have to be willing to challenge our own assumptions about what it means to be an educational leader. We must be willing to listen to the voices of marginalized communities and center their experiences in our decision-making processes and take risks and experiment with new approaches, even if they are not immediately successful.

Reflection Questions

- How does our vision for the future challenge the status quo?
- Can I identify my mental models that get in the way of a better future?
- Do I know where the positive deviants are in my school or district?
- How am I creating a safe and inclusive space that respects diverse perspectives and encourages open dialogue?
- How can I create opportunities for dialogue, such as focus groups, town hall meetings, or student-led forums, where participants can share their visions and aspirations for the future?
- What collaborative structures (such as advisory committees or task forces, where students, teachers, parents, and community members can work together to co-create a shared vision and goals) exist or need to be created?
- How am I thinking differently about goals?

CHAPTER 5

Beliefs About Change and About People

Any sort of change involves, at some level, asking people to do things differently. And the repeating motif of change in the reform-heavy field of education means that educators are being asked to do a lot of changing. Whether or not they actually change what they do is another matter; we are often privy to conversations about how any given change is or is not going according to plan, and we hear the explanations for why that's the case. The explanations frequently follow the same template: At the school level, equity-minded leaders with righteous visions of success for all are thwarted in their efforts to enact improvements by teachers who are resistant to change, lack the will and skill, are frightened of change, or don't have a growth mindset. Or there is a district-level variant: Superintendents and central office leaders are dismayed by the lack of change at a school level and complain that school leaders just don't possess a great enough sense of urgency—the implication being, of course, that the central office leaders are not deficient in that quality.

We understand that these characterizations on our part are cartoonish, and a little cynical. We employ them nevertheless because they allow us to make several points. First, these explanations simply lack power; the psychology of change encompasses a huge body of research, and very little of that work makes it into these simple accounts. Second, it seems unlikely that so many educators are daunted by the idea of change while their superiors are not; this perpetuates the unhelpful mental model that there are strategists (usually principals and superintendents) who devise clever plans, and there are implementers (principals and teachers) who are charged with executing the plans but avoid doing so when arduous or inconvenient. And third, explanations that have to do with the will and skill of the person ignore all the literature that demonstrates that the setting in which the person works is a potent influence on the person's behavior.

And just to be clear, we have decades of experience between us, and we know that some people really are jerks—we just don't think that this should be the default explanation for why people are sometimes slow to do what they are being asked to do. In this chapter we consider some of the research in social and organizational psychology that helps explain the challenges of change, the mental models that humans hold that frequently make change less likely, and how overcoming these challenges may have more to do with looking at the whole system with a view to changing the conditions in which change is expected to happen rather than the characteristics of those expected to change. We describe several constructs from social and organizational psychology that provide greater nuance in describing what makes people more or less willing to change and that do not idolize or demonize them based on their choices.

One of the phrases we hear most often when leaders are talking about implementing plans is that "change is scary" or its slightly milder variant "change is hard." Further probing generally exposes that leaders expect that most teachers will be resistant to change—at least to some degree. We take issue with this framing, not because it's always false, but because it puts the onus on others to overcome their fear and summon the strength to do what's right for kids. This absolves leaders from doing their part in making transitions as smooth as possible for all involved, while not blaming others for their concerns about making change.

Further, if leaders initiate a change expecting that others will resist changing their practices, then their expectations for the change to be successful are reduced. This may make them less willing to invest their own time and resources in supporting the change. Also, if they think change is going to involve some measure of conflict, that too may make them less likely to engage with making the change, as they may be unwilling to expend relational capital on an effort that they don't expect, consciously or unconsciously, will be successful—or they may be simply conflict-averse.

We often hear another reason for change to be stymied, and that is culture. We hear educators talking about culture as though it is alive, with agency, as in, "The culture here won't support that," or "The school culture is risk-averse," or "We don't have a culture of trust in this district." This use of the word culture represents the hypostatizing of an abstract idea in a way that is profoundly unhelpful because it signals that there is an immutable force acting in opposition to positive change. Culture is the word that is given to the beliefs people hold about what it takes to be successful in an organization. We don't argue that this definition makes culture easier to change, but it does bring it within the control of leaders, because it is they who influence the beliefs of the members of the organization about what brings about success.

Additionally, we find it ironic that so much blame is placed on people for being unwilling to change their behavior, which seems like a lot of deficit thinking when one of the things that educational leaders complain about the most is what they perceive to be deficit thinking in others. A theme throughout this book is that equity advocates and improvers acknowledge that individual actors play a role but that the system is producing predictable patterns of behavior. If we know, for example, that for any given reform initiative, a certain percentage of teachers will lead the way and a certain percentage may never change, then the wise approach is to look at the system that is generating that pattern rather than simply praise the innovators and excoriate the laggards (Rogers, 1995).

Sometimes, people really do resist change, but they do it for good reasons. They may question the motives behind the change; they may not believe that the change will pay off in terms of desired outcomes; they may believe that the resources needed to support the change are insufficient or otherwise inadequate; they may believe that the change will increase rather than reduce inequity or disparity; or many other reasons that have nothing to do with fear, effort, or skill. The number of changes that educators could be asked to make in a year, let alone a career, are innumerable; one of the beneficial side effects of improvement science is that it focuses attention on one measurable change at a time; therefore, the change being studied may happen more rapidly, but the overall effect is to limit churn, or too many changes at once.

Some of these constructs concern an individual's attributes, but it would be a mistake to place all the weight of explanation at an individual level. Rather, the broader organizational attributes are very powerful, and changes at that level often provide traction in bringing about improvement. Making change in service of equity is hard enough in the best of circumstances, so it only makes sense to approach change armed with knowledge about what is most likely to support improvement, and much of that has to do less with people's individual attributes and more with the way humans tend to think and the conditions in which they work.

ATTRIBUTION

One of the most common biases to which humans are liable is that we attribute results to individuals that more properly belong to the situation in which those individuals operate (Ross & Nisbett, 2011). For example, the marshmallow test is a classic experiment in psychology in which young children are presented with a marshmallow, which they may eat, but they are told that if they can wait a few minutes without eating, the tester will leave the room and return with an additional marshmallow (Mischel, 1974). Later in the lives of these original children, comparison was made between their ability to refrain from eating the marshmallow, known as delayed gratification, and other measures of accomplishment, leading to the conclusion that self-control is "the engine of success" (Mischel, 2014). The clear and profound message is that the ability to delay gratification is an uncomplicated signal that the child has the capacity for self-control, which is an innate trait or personality characteristic.

Subsequent experiments have shown, however, that the marshmallow test is not a reliable measure of self-control as a personal trait. If the marshmallow test is administered after a similar test in which children are told that they can use crayons to draw, but if they wait a few minutes, the researcher will leave and return with fancier art supplies, and the researcher returns without the promised nicer supplies, the children are much more likely to eat the first marshmallow (Kidd et al., 2013). They have learned that, in this particular situation, delaying gratification is not worth it; the researcher cannot be relied on to make good on the promise that waiting will be rewarded. This throws the whole premise of the marshmallow test into doubt, because if it turns out that what the marshmallow test is really measuring is the child's belief in the reliability of the environment to behave as advertised, then eating the first marshmallow is actually the more logical choice for children whose experience of life is that adults cannot be relied on or that conditions can change very quickly and unpredictably.

Decades of research in social psychology have demonstrated that humans make causal attributions to personality and discount the influence of setting in explaining the behavior of others, but do the opposite when explaining their own behavior when the outcome is negative (Culcea, 2017). In other words, we tend to take credit for desired outcomes and attribute them to our own intelligence, experience, or skill, but when things don't go well, we blame the conditions, the actions of others, or just bad luck. The overestimation of personality in explaining the behavior of others is known as the fundamental attribution error.

The fundamental attribution error is also at work when racism is under discussion; it is politically expedient to chalk up racist incidents such as racially or religiously motivated mass shootings to the actions of a mentally disturbed person or an evil racist, rather than interpret those actions as a product of societal conditions. The stance of the political right that racism is an individual trait rather than a feature of the system is a feature of the defensive routines around race that we discuss later.

We see the fundamental attribution error play out all the time in our work lives. A superintendent complains about the lack of courage of principals in discussing equity with teachers but explains that he cannot have such a discussion with the school board because politically it's a contentious issue and he doesn't want to expose any divisions in the board at the moment. A principal asserts that the goals that teachers set themselves during the teacher evaluation process betray their low expectations for students of color and students receiving special education services but explains the school goals that are written in the school improvement plan in terms of making the school look good in the eyes of parents. An instructional coach ascribes teachers' unwillingness to be coached to their lack of interest in their own professional growth but explains that his own unwillingness to participate in a peer coaching program is because it is not set up to support coaches who have, like him, more experience.

Our experience in schools is that there are many constructs that are treated as though they are features of the individual rather than the environment, and the absence thereof is invoked to explain low achievement: grit, intrinsic motivation, commitment. We encourage educators to think of these constructs as being states, rather than traits, that are a product of the environment (Liljedahl, 2020). Or, as Black & Wiliam (1998a) phrase the same idea, we need to stop thinking about these constructs as inputs and start seeing them as outcomes. This is a very useful heuristic when working both with children and adults.

Knowledge of the attribution bias is important because educators need to be aware that what they frequently attribute to the beliefs, actions, or personalities of individuals are actually evidence of the system at work. Knowing that people's actions are much more likely to be influenced by, or in response to, the conditions in which they work is actually empowering, because the conditions, and the system itself, is amenable to change, whereas it is difficult to imagine how to go about changing someone's personality. The following factors that are certainly relevant in managing change should be viewed in light of the points we have just made about culture and attribution bias. To be more specific, these factors are important, but they do not explain as much of the likelihood that change will happen as the environmental factors, which are frequently known as culture, that are present.

DEFENSIVE ROUTINES

As we noted earlier, not all unwillingness to change is a manifestation of resistance, fear, or obstinacy; sometimes the change itself has not been well thought through or adequately communicated, and we consider those situations later in the chapter. But sometimes, unwillingness to change is a kind of self-protection. People are highly motivated to feel competent (Elliot & Dweck, 2005) and are aware and sensitive to threats to their sense of themselves as adequate (Cohen & Sherman, 2014). Defensive reasoning is the typical human response to situations in which that sense of adequacy is challenged. We experience, or fear that we might experience, embarrassment, humiliation, ostracism, shame, or other emotions that come into play under three conditions: We believe we are being judged, we believe that we may be found wanting, and the standard by which we are judged matters to us, frequently because social cost is attached to deficiency. Defensive behaviors, which we mostly perform unconsciously, are intended to maintain our sense of control; maximize winning and minimize losing; relieve unwelcome and unpleasant emotions; and to still behave rationally—in other words, to not look like we are being defensive, even though that's exactly what we are (Argyris, 1994).

There are many typical defensive behaviors: denying that we did something, denying that what we did was wrong or substandard, denying the validity of the standard, attacking the credibility of the source, attacking the motive of the source, arguing that there has been a mistake or a misunderstanding, arguing that there is something more important at stake, avoiding the conversation entirely by getting upset, and ending the conversation by walking away or even by physically attacking the source. These efforts at self-protection come at a cost, because they frequently interfere with our internalizing information that might be helpful to us—in other words, they protect us from feedback, even when the feedback is accurate. Our response to feedback frequently has more to do with how we feel about it than with how useful it is.

Defensive behaviors can be seen clearly and often in two arenas in education: evaluation and equity. Educator evaluation has long been a source of tension; it is as if it was designed to engender the greatest amount of defensiveness by basing a high-stakes rating of someone's competence on a small portion of the work they do in situations where many of the outcomes on which they are being evaluated are influenced by factors outside of their control. We know from years' worth of coaching workshops that supervisors and coaches are under the impression that if they could only be better messengers of feedback, then teachers would not display so many defensive behaviors. We argue that the conditions under which these conversations take place—under the very long shadow of evaluation—are actually the problem.

Supervisors frequently comment that they would rather be working with new teachers, because new teachers are grateful for, and responsive to, feedback. And this may be true, because it is socially acceptable for a new educator to be less than expert—indeed, it could be argued that the role of rookie is a well-established one in education, and the new teacher is playing an important part in the everyday life of schools by submitting to socialization from fellow educators and to mentoring from supervisors (Goffman, 1959). More senior educators, however, are supposed to be proficient at their jobs, and so the evaluation leads to self-protection. Further, the way that most evaluation systems are structured, it is in the best interests of educators to be seen at their best, because the judgment of their performance is entered into the permanent record. If we were really interested in supporting educators' professional growth, we would make it worth their while to be seen at their worst, because then they would be more likely to receive support that would help them to get better.

Workshops, data meetings, and coaching focused on equity are also highly liable to produce defensive reasoning among educators, especially but not exclusively White educators. The kinds of behaviors that DiAngelo describes in *White Fragility* (2018) are predictable, although sometimes extreme, avoidance behaviors, designed to protect the people displaying them from a challenge to their sense of themselves as good people. To be accused of racism and, just as importantly, to confront the possibility that one might be racist are almost guaranteed to elicit defensive reactions, because racism is highly socially stigmatized; being accused of racism is one of the most shaming prospects that a White person can face (Pollock, 2004). Likewise, to consider themselves as racist may be the greatest challenge to their sense of themselves as decent human beings that many White people have faced.

During the summer we are writing this book, much of the United States is in the middle of a massive defensive routine. In order for certain citizens to be protected from "discomfort," and so that White students will not feel "guilt" for being White, legislatures in various parts of the country have banned the teaching of various race-related concepts, particularly critical race theory. The same template is being used as for any defensive routine. Some White citizens perceive that a particular act, in this case discussion of racism, presents a threat to their sense of themselves and/or their institutions as being morally adequate. These citizens wish to avoid the emotions—in this case, guilt and outrage. So, they engage a mechanism to avoid the threat by legislating speech acts that imply that racism is anything other than beliefs held by racist individuals. They further deny that defensive routines are in play; this can happen in a variety of ways, including accusing the "woke left" of imposing its "woke ideology" on others, denying that there is such a thing as systemic racism, and accusing anyone who suggests that the United States of America has been and continues to be a racist country of being unpatriotic.

If we want people to be more open to feedback, to be more willing to experiment in improving their practice, and to be able to engage in conversations about equity, then the most practical ways to do that are first to lower the stakes that are in effect by taking away judgment, and second to acknowledge the systemic nature of the inequity under consideration. Obviously, this is actually incredibly difficult to do.

BIAS AND PSYCHOLOGICAL DISTANCE

We think it helps to start with the premise that everyone is racist—a point that Ibram Kendi (2019) makes in *How to Be an Antiracist*—and also sexist and ableist. Further, the idea that racism—personal, institutional, or systemic—or any other bias can be eradicated through awareness or consciousness-raising is not well-supported by research. It is not actually the case that just because you know better, you do better (Kristal & Santos, 2021). Knowledge of the nature of bias, mindfulness and self-awareness, time, empathy, interactions with others less like ourselves, and the goal of reducing our own biases can lead to less biased action, more prosocial behavior, and better decision-making, but not to the *elimination* of bias. We are also heavily influenced by those around us—one of the most interesting features of racism is how geographically localized it is and that people become less racist when they move from a racist part of the country to a less racist part of the country, and vice versa.

Bias is a very human condition. We are sensitive to a host of characteristics, including skin color, facial features, hair color, religion, dis/ability, gender identity, sexual orientation, age, social class, nationality, and political affiliation, and we make finer distinctions based on, for example, affiliation with an alma mater or sports team. Our biases result from explicit and implicit messages we have received over the course of our lifetimes that have taught us that these characteristics have meaning: Women with this hair color are ditzy, people with this skin color are likely to be criminals, men who support this sports team are idiots, people of this religion are avaricious (Banaji & Greenwald, 2016). We have all been brought up with mental models that socialize us to believe that people of Northern European descent are superior intellectually and culturally, and even though the fact that race is only a social construct and has no basis in biology has been well established, that social construct still holds a lot of power. We have biases regarding body composition that affect women and people of color in particular. We have also been socialized to see men as saviors and women, people of color, the elderly, and the differently abled as in need of saving. And we tend to think of poverty as deserved—that if poor people were smarter, worked harder, or just believed more in their dreams, that they would not be poor. In the same way that we conflate poverty with character, we confound other physical characteristics with innate traits: height in men with competence, physical attractiveness with intelligence, and body composition with self-control.

Psychological distance is the term used to describe the perceived separation or dissimilarity between individuals and other individuals, objects, or events (Trope & Liberman, 2010). Psychological distance can be measured in terms of time (the further in the future, the less psychologically salient), distance (other parts of the world and places that we perceive as remote are less psychologically salient), or social distance (the less someone is like me, the greater the psychological distance). Clarity and precision also matter; vague ideas are less psychologically salient than specific actions. The implications of this are truly far-reaching. Events that are far in the future are psychologically distant, and we perceive them as less likely to happen, and this affects our decision-making—for example, while climate change is seen as something that is going to happen at some point in the future or to affect people in other countries, it is much harder to rally support for changing policies that might mitigate the impact of climate change.

There are two implications of psychological distance that have the greatest impact on equity and improvement science. First, because people who are socially different (including but not limited to race and socioeconomic status) from us are psychologically distant from us, it is harder to empathize with them and harder to take their concerns seriously when their experience varies from our own. This is a major concern when decision-makers are disproportionately White, male, able-bodied, and middle class. Their biases are magnified by psychological distance. Second, when plans are written that are vague in terms of action and distant in terms of time frame, it is much harder to organize people to make changes. The combined issues of bias and psychological distance represent an important opportunity for educators with expertise in equity work and improvement science. Equity work includes education on bias and how that impacts our plans and decision-making. Improvement work includes being specific about immediate action with very short time frames. The two in combination make change much more likely to be successful. We have other guidance for educators to reduce psychological distance across several dimensions:

1. Keep your language informal: Use colloquial language, avoid the passive tense, use people's names rather than honorifics and titles.
2. Keep the focus on the very near future—what can be accomplished in the next week?
3. Be specific about who is doing what. Clarify what is expected from people in different roles, which makes the work more immediate for them and, therefore, less psychologically distant.
4. Communicate details. The more concrete, the more real it seems and the more likely to happen: details about what's going to happen, how something is going to be done, who's going to be involved, and so on.
5. Tell stories. We feel more psychological distance from people we are socially distant from—sometimes that's about physical distance, but it's also about features like race, religion, and class. Stories about that provide specific details about individual children and families and provide a better picture of what their lives are actually like, thereby closing psychological distance.

MINDSETS

Another idea that we hear a lot when the topic of change, or failure to change, comes up is the idea of mindset. Mindset is a person's beliefs about their own psychology; it is, in other words, a mental model about our own minds, including what we think we are capable of; how we judge ourselves; the way we frame what happens to us (for example, whether we think we are lucky, whether we think we get what we deserve in life, and whether we believe that God has a plan for us); whether we see our capabilities as innate traits or learned skills; and so on. There are three particular mindsets that we focus on here, because they have been studied extensively and are useful constructs for thinking about the human side of change: fixed/growth mindset, perceived self-efficacy (PSE), and stereotype threat.

Mindset has been popularized by the work of Carol Dweck, and particularly her work on the concept of fixed and growth mindset (Dweck, 2000). The premise is that people tend to believe one of two things about their own abilities. People with a fixed mindset believe that intelligence, or any other trait, is predetermined and not malleable. People with a growth mindset believe that intelligence is "cultivated through effort"—in other words, you become more intelligent as you learn. This basic distinction has a cascade of consequences. From the answers to a set of questions designed to determine whether a person has a fixed or growth mindset, they (and therefore we) can predict how that person will behave in many different situations. For example, when given a test when they don't know all the answers, the growth mindset person pays more attention to the corrections than the fixed mindset person does, because the growth mindset person believes that the feedback can help them become smarter. When given feedback, the fixed mindset person can react defensively or be hurt and humiliated, because for them, what they can currently do is a reflection of all they can be.

The growth mindset person sees many risks as an opportunity to learn, an opportunity to become better at something, a chance to be stronger. A fixed mindset person doesn't see the benefit in risk, because failure would be a negative reflection on their intelligence. The fixed mindset person is proudest of achievement, whereas the growth mindset person is proudest of effort. Effort, therefore, is only for people who need to try hard because they won't succeed any other way. Lack of effort, on the other hand, can be a convenient excuse for a fixed mindset person—"I could have done it if I'd tried" is a useful explanation for not succeeding at something while protecting their view of their ability. A fixed mindset does not value effort—"If I am smart, I don't need to try." The fixed mindset person has to explain failure so that they do not have to conclude that they are not smart. Their way of coping with not coping is to blame others or the particular circumstances in which the failure occurred. Dweck (2006) chronicles all the excuses John McEnroe gives in his autobiography for all the matches he did not win—the common thread is that it was never his fault. The growth mindset person doesn't have these issues—quite the opposite: They are likely to see failures as the learning experiences on which successes are built.

This description of the differences between fixed and growth mindsets sets them up in contrast with each other, whereas in reality our beliefs about ourselves do not fit into such neat categories. Also, mindsets themselves are not fixed; our beliefs about ourselves are subject to change and may also differ across domains of endeavor. For example, I may have a growth mindset about my intelligence and see how I get smarter in response to reading, dialogue, and other forms of intellectual stimulation. However, I may not see my creativity or my athletic ability in the same way and do nothing to improve because I believe it would be pointless to do so.

Our concern with mindsets is not with Dweck's definitions or her research more generally, but in how we hear it applied. We frequently hear supervisors speak of those whom they supervise as "having a fixed mindset." We infer that they may mean different things by this. One meaning is that educators, especially teachers, are risk-averse; they are not willing to try new things, especially the practices that have been the topic of professional development sessions at a school or district. Another similar meaning is that teachers are not self-reflective, or responsive to feedback, because they seem unwilling to change their practices. Another is that they think that teachers believe that intelligence is determined at birth, and therefore students whom they perceive as less intelligent cannot be expected to meet high standards; in this usage, a teacher's fixed mindset is synonymous with having low expectations for some students.

These scenarios are problematic for several reasons. First, supervisors display beliefs about teachers that they would decry if they heard teachers make such remarks about students; we often hear comments that teachers "need to have a growth mindset," as if this was a trait with a causal relationship with student outcomes. Second, in failing to understand that mindsets are beliefs about ourselves ("self-theories" in Dweck's language), diagnosing the mindsets of others perpetuates the paternalistic view of the supervisor as knowing what others are like, knowing why they behave the way they do, being entitled to pass judgment on them, and knowing what is best for them.

Dweck's work on fixed and growth mindsets shows that our beliefs about ourselves have a powerful influence on the way we think and behave and overlap with the identities we adopt. The term identity, like so many others in this chapter, is used in many different ways. We hear the term used in the work we do with schools and districts, and the more marginalized the students, the more that the term is invoked—the term is associated with students of color (racial identity) and queer students (sexual identity) in the same way that race is often seen to apply only to students of color and not to White students. Some aspects of identity are seen to be more firmly attached than others: race, religion, gender, sexuality. Some are socially grounded: the football team you support, the swimming pool you belong to, the neighborhood where you grew up. Some are considered individual, as when you think of yourself as a writer, or an athlete, or a parent. We write about this more in Chapter 2.

SELF-EFFICACY AND STEREOTYPE THREAT

PSE refers to an individual's belief in their ability to perform a specific task or achieve a particular outcome in a particular context. When faced with a task, our PSE is determined by our answers to two simple questions: Can I do this? and If I do this, will I get the desired outcome? PSE became an important construct in education after the publication of a Rand Corporation study on the success of reading programs in Los Angeles (Armor et al., 1976). In studying the factors that contributed to the programs' successes, two items on a teacher questionnaire were very highly correlated with student achievement, and those two questions measured the teachers' beliefs about their ability to effect improvement in the educational attainment of their students. After this, PSE and its cousin, collective efficacy, have featured prominently in the literature on educational reform.

People with high PSE will try harder and persist longer than those who do not because they believe that their efforts will pay off. Over time, this leads to efficacy–performance spirals (Lindsley et al., 1995): Belief that effort will lead to success leads a person to try hard and take more risks; trying hard and taking more risks leads to more learning and more success; more learning and more success reinforce the person's belief that hard work and risk-taking will pay off, leading to more hard work and risk-taking; and so on. It is a self-reinforcing cycle. It is, of course, just as likely to be on the downward slope of the spiral: Lack of belief that a person will be successful means that they do not bother to try; therefore, they do not experience success, further reinforcing their lack of belief in their own capacity.

Stereotype threat is a related idea. Steele (2010) documents some of the very many stereotypes in play for people with a variety of identity markers and how they impact the performance of people who are stereotyped. Our interpretation of the mechanism is that when you are in a situation where a stereotype is in play, and you are implicated in that stereotype because of your socialized identity, and you care about the outcome, then concern about affirming that stereotype impedes your performance because it takes up cognitive resources and it suppresses your perceived self-efficacy. For many students, it is less stressful and simply easier to not put forth any effort than to try and fail and, simultaneously, confirm a stereotype that you are aware includes you.

Bandura provides several ways of improving perceived self-efficacy: experiencing success, seeing others close to me succeed, encouragement, and one's own mindset. We advocate that improvement science with an equity lens would pay particular attention to ensuring that marginalized students experience success, not draw attention to stereotypes that are present for them, and work particularly hard on providing them with a sense of belonging and a belief that their teachers have faith in their ability (Yeager et al., 2014).

IDENTITY

Norman Maclean, who is best known for writing *A River Runs Through It*, wrote a book about the Mann Gulch disaster called *Young Men and Fire* (Maclean, 1992). In August 1949, a team of firefighters parachuted into an area of Montana known as Mann Gulch to fight a fire that had started the day before. Conditions were "explosive," and within 2 hours the crew had to run for their lives, running uphill to stay ahead of the flames, but they were overrun, despite the admonition by the crew chief to drop their tools and step into the escape fire that he created by setting alight the grass in front of them. The crew leader survived by lying down in the ashes of the fire he had made. The rest of the crew ran for the ridge, but only 2 made it, and the other 13 men were killed. This story was used in several articles by Karl Weick (1993, 2007), who suggested that in the case of firefighters, their tools are so much a part of who they are that they cannot let them go; to drop their tools, even in the face of imminent death, is to give up a part of themselves that they cannot conceive letting go. Weick's point is that to ask someone to metaphorically drop their tools is akin to asking them to give up who they are.

Asking teachers to give up practices that they may equate with their identity as teachers may be challenging. These practices vary, but could include grading, assigning homework, and helping students whom teachers perceive as less able. One of the districts with which we work runs a professional learning opportunity in the summer; one of the goals is to encourage teachers to give up practices that they perceive as teaching, including helping out struggling students, not asking challenging questions of students whom teachers perceive as low-achieving, and not cold-calling or engaging in other practices that the teachers think will make the students uncomfortable. All this maps onto equity because the students whom teachers want to rescue from embarrassment or feeling awkward are almost, by definition, marginalized students. In order to make it possible for teachers to give up these practices, which they perceive as being helpful, the professional development includes watching demonstration teachers who employ alternate practices and asking the students to give their feedback during a student focus group toward the end of the week. Seeing the more challenging practices and hearing students talk about how they wish that all teachers employed them gives teachers a bridge to changing their own practices, but also to changing their identity.

MOTIVATION

On American TV detective shows, the word "motive" is used all the time; it is the reason why someone would commit a crime—usually murder, as isn't that what most detective shows are about? Motive, in this sense, is the reason why someone makes a particular choice. It can be a feeling: rage, envy, desire. Or it can be a cause such as financial gain, punishment, or to cover up another crime. In acting, the word motivation is used in a similar way: What factors move the character to behave as they do? In both examples, motivation is specific to the setting.

In education, the word motivation is used a great deal, but it is often used in a different sense. In education, we speak of teachers and students as "being motivated," as though it is a personality trait or a state of being, indicating willingness to put forth effort. We speak of "losing motivation" as though it is something someone possesses, rather than simply a stimulus to action. We attach valence to motivation; motivated students are equated with high achievement, and therefore low-achieving students are seen as lacking motivation or as lazy.

In addition, some types of motivation seem to be more highly valued than others. In particular, we often hear the phrase "intrinsic motivation" as a desirable trait, as in "we want students to be intrinsically motivated." Often, however, this means that educators want students to be intrinsically motivated to do the things that the educators want them to do, rather than the things that they want to do, which undermines the whole concept of intrinsic motivation; students who are intrinsically motivated to maintain their social relationships, for example, are often chastised for not taking their studies seriously enough. We are often in the position of hearing educators bemoaning students' lack of agency, when it actually appears to be the last thing that educators want them to have. Frequently, it is the most marginalized students who are most often seen as the least motivated.

Further, motivation, or lack thereof, is frequently viewed as a contributing factor to the success or failure of a particular change initiative. We contend that the problem with thinking about motivation as a permanent condition is that it places the responsibility for success or failure on the personality of certain individuals, which has the corollary of removing responsibility from others, usually leaders, and from poorly conceptualized or implemented change initiatives.

All this is to say that we need to have better ways of thinking and talking about motivation—ones that don't demonize people who think or behave differently and that support changes in service of marginalized students. Here is a simple heuristic for thinking about motivation that relies on creating the conditions rather than relying on intrinsic motivation.

If you want people to be motivated to do something, then they (not you!) must:

1. Understand what it is they are being asked to do.
2. Believe that they are capable of doing it and that doing it will have the desired result (perceived self-efficacy).
3. Believe that there will be enough time to master this new aspect of their craft before some other urgent request supplants it.
4. Believe that making the change will be worth it.

GOALS AND ACCOUNTABILITY

Account is an old word, going back to the early 1300s, and has slightly different meanings, but the core idea is transparency; you can account for your whereabouts, you can account for how money was spent, you can account for your reasons for doing something. The word accountable appears in the late 1500s in the sense of being charged with showing how or why something happened or that you have discharged your duties. And the word accountability appears in the late 1700s, in Vermont, actually, with the connotation of showing that you have done what was required of you. And in modern education, accountability has moved beyond transparency and fulfilling your obligations to also taking responsibility for the results of your actions—not merely doing what you were supposed to do—and also being rewarded or punished for those results. A detailed history of school accountability can be found in Figlio and Loeb (2011).

To be clear, we are not suggesting that accountability is all bad. We think that data on student performance should be available. We think that educational institutions should be required to make their decisions, financial and otherwise, public. We also acknowledge that accountability appears to have improved test scores, especially in math, although it is not clear that gaps in achievement among student groups have decreased (Figlio & Loeb, 2011). In other words, we believe in accountability in the sense of transparency. Our concerns about accountability lie in the implications for disabling or enabling change that will benefit marginalized students, especially when accountability means that rewards and punishments land on individuals. We also discuss other implications of test-based accountability in Chapter 7.

Accountability for individuals shows up most clearly in educator evaluation. The theory of action here is that if educators know that they are going to be judged, at least in some part, by the results that they achieve, then those results will increase. The supposed mechanism that connects evaluation and results is not always clear. It could be that the presence of evaluation will cause educators to work harder, although that assumes that they will work harder at doing the right things, which assumes that they know the right thing to do. It could be that evaluation will focus educators' attention on what the policy that governs evaluation—directly or indirectly—values, as expressed by what is measured, although that risks the unintended consequence that the measures will lose some of their value—see Chapter 7. And it could be that the presence of rewards and punishments will incentivize educators to figure out how to better achieve the performance goals that are being measured.

The operation of educator evaluation hinges in part on establishing goals that educators are "held accountable" for meeting—the role of measurement is to establish whether those goals have been met. Whatever mechanism is posited to explain the relationship between accountability and results, knowledge of goals is integral. Goals are so important in educator evaluation that it is easy to conclude that the goals themselves are assumed to have agency; this probably stems from the heavy emphasis on "Big Hairy Audacious Goals" (BHAGs) in Collins's book *Good to Great* (2001). This emphasis on goals has chilling effects on teacher behavior. It is in teachers' best interest to set goals that they are confident that they will achieve, because that means that their evaluation rating is less at risk, and the reason that they are confident that they can achieve these goals is because they already know how to achieve them, which means doing what they are already doing.

If it is not the case that teachers set a "safe" goal, perhaps because they are required to set a "stretch" goal, then attaching a rating to the achievement of that goal also affects behavior. Such a goal is known as a performance goal; it requires the achievement of a fixed, measurable outcome, such as a certain percentage of students meeting a certain target, like a score on a standardized reading test. If the goal is a performance goal, this will increase performance only if the person charged with meeting the goal knows everything they need to know in order to meet it. This is because, as the literature on performance goals and learning goals shows (Seijts et al., 2004), giving people outcome goals that they do not already know how to meet encourages them to try many different ideas for change, which they abandon when they are not immediately successful. This pattern of behavior is recognizable in the description in Garner et al. (2017) of teacher teams attempting to bring up student scores in the weeks before the high-stakes test their students are about to take.

If Deming (1982) is right and people are, in almost all cases, already doing the best they know how to do, then the focus on performance goals that has been a feature of educator evaluation since the launch of Race to the Top should not, for the most part, have led to a measurable increase in student performance, in line with the research on performance goals. And indeed, the most comprehensive review so far of the impact of teacher evaluation (Bleiberg et al., 2021) shows no discernible effect of state teacher evaluation reforms on student achievement in mathematics or language arts. (The exceptions to these findings were in districts that differed substantially from the norm—for example, the Washington, DC IMPACT system resulted in the dismissal of a "nontrivial" number of teachers who received below-acceptable performance ratings, which is not the case across the country.)

Learning goals, in contrast with performance goals, reflect a desire to help educators improve their practice rather than to measure their current performance. Learning goals encourage focusing on the mechanism to achieve a target, rather than turning the target into a goal. The attention of the individual being asked to meet the goal is directed at studying and improving their practice, and as a result they are much more likely to be strategic in the way in which they go about improving. This approach is exactly analogous to the implementation of plan-do-study-act (PDSA) cycles, which entails strategically choosing a change idea that is implemented methodically in order to learn from each short cycle of improvement. It is also in line with the other learner-centered approaches to adult learning, such as action research.

PSYCHOLOGICAL SAFETY

The research of Amy Edmondson (2012, 2018) shows how important it is that members of an organization believe that they are psychologically safe: that making honest mistakes, taking risks in the service of their own learning, and speaking truth to power are both expected and supported by the organization. Psychological safety means that the organization puts itself in a position to learn from the work of its members, whether they are learning as a by-product of their daily tasks or as part of a designed experiment. A lack of psychological safety means that workers will be less likely to confess to making mistakes, will hide failures, and are generally motivated to protect themselves against real or perceived repercussions.

It is worth noting that making mistakes often represents high risk because women and people of color are under stereotype threat of various types: appearing less intelligent, lazy, weak, indecisive, or incompetent. Additionally, many strategic choices to change direction or abandon a project may appear to be mistakes because they are filtered through negative stereotypes, when those same actions may be laudable when carried out by a White man. There are many books, articles, and podcasts featuring the benefits of "failing fast" and "failing forward," but this space tends to be dominated by White men.

AT YOUR DESK OR IN THE HALLS

In this chapter we ask you to accept that many of the ideas you may have been taught about why people do or do not change are wrong, or at least misguided or incomplete. In many respects, we ask you to consider that the ability to change has less to do with individual traits and much more to do with the situations in which people live and work. We hope that you choose to embrace the possibility that what you think you know may be more limited than you realize and that it is worth it to cultivate the humility to think more expansively about the many possibilities for interpretation that exist in any given situation.

Reflection Questions

- What stories do I typically tell myself to explain people's resistance to change? How should I think differently?
- How do context and situation shape people's behaviors? What is my role in creating contexts or situations that support the changes I am leading?
- How can I create conditions that reduce the likelihood of defensive routines?
- How can I combat psychological distance and help others engage more empathetically?

CHAPTER 6

Dismantling Traditional Power Structures

Dr. Manny Ramirez was the chief academic officer in a sprawling suburban district. Over the course of his 10-year tenure, the district had undergone a significant demographic shift, with an influx of students of color and those from lower socioeconomic backgrounds. Manny was renowned for his scholarly prowess and deep understanding of educational theories.

As the district evolved, concerns arose about the growing achievement gap and the need for culturally responsive pedagogy. Faculty members and administrators noticed that certain student groups were consistently lagging behind. Seeking guidance, they invited Manny to address these pressing issues. During his visit, he passionately delivered an academic discourse on a single learning theory he believed held the key to educational success. He attributed the achievement gap to a supposed deficiency in applying this theory across classrooms. Despite the audience's attempts to bring up broader challenges stemming from socioeconomic disparities, language barriers, and cultural insensitivity, Manny remained steadfast in his conviction.

Dr. Ramirez dismissed their concerns as distractions, emphasizing that a rigorous adherence to his chosen theory was the panacea for all educational disparities. He left the district with an air of intellectual superiority, leaving behind a room full of frustrated educators who had hoped for practical solutions to their complex challenges. Over time, it became clear that Manny's theoretical approach failed to bridge the growing divide among students. The district's changing demographics demanded a more nuanced understanding of the multifaceted barriers faced by marginalized communities. Dr. Ramirez's unwavering commitment to his favored theory hindered meaningful progress and highlighted the dangers of clinging to one perspective while disregarding the broader context.

We have worked with many leaders like Manny over the years, and it's likely that you have too. People in power tend to think they are right, not because they are always right, but because they have power (Flyvbjerg, 1998). Powerful people in Western society—almost all of them White, straight men—have a long history of dismissing the valid complaints of the marginalized and disenfranchised by infantilizing people from poverty, people of color, and women and blaming them for their own status and by rationalizing their own power over others. In the pursuit of equity in education, educators must critically examine and challenge the traditional power structures that have long perpetuated inequality. This chapter describes the necessity for dismantling traditional power structures when improvement for equity is the goal because knowledge of how a system works is not located in one part of the system, and neither is knowledge of how to improve a system.

TRADITIONAL POWER STRUCTURES

Several years ago, a 7th-grade teacher was sharing his frustration with his district's hyperfocus on improving test scores for Black, Indigenous, People of Color (BIPOC) students and the lack of resources available to make a significant impact: "If the achievement gap was reversed and White students' scores were lower, people would throw tons of money at the problem." While we understand his position, we disagree. We believe that if White students were consistently scoring below their BIPOC classmates on achievement tests, those in power would change the test.

Power is generally understood as the ability or capacity to influence others, make decisions, and shape the direction of an organization or educational system. It involves relationships, resources, and the exercise of authority within specific social, cultural, and institutional contexts. English et al. (2010) describe power as "the ability of individuals or groups to mobilize resources to accomplish goals" (p. 301). This definition highlights the idea that power involves the mobilization of resources, which can include knowledge, expertise, positions of authority, and social connections, among others. Another influential perspective on power in educational leadership is offered by Leithwood et al. (2006), who conceptualize power as "the capacity to produce intended effects on others or on the environment" (p. 9). They emphasize the productive nature of power and how it can influence individuals, groups, and organizational systems to achieve desired outcomes.

In both cases, the definition of power is tied to the actions of a person and is understood as a dynamic and relational phenomenon that is enacted through the actions and behaviors of individuals or groups. Power is not an inanimate "thing" that you keep on your bookshelf. An individual's power is exercised and demonstrated through specific actions, decisions, and interactions. This view recognizes that power is not simply a personal attribute or possession that one possesses, but rather emerges in social contexts and is contingent on relationships and social dynamics. Power is enacted through individuals' behaviors, choices, and interactions with others, which can have tangible effects on the distribution of resources, decision-making processes, and the shaping of outcomes within a given context.

Because the notion of power is so closely tied to the actions of a person, it is easy to conflate power with leadership, which can be problematic, as it obscures the distinct nature of these concepts and their implications for individuals, organizations, and society. This conflation often leads to a narrow and simplistic understanding of leadership solely based on the exercise of power and authority, disregarding the multifaceted dimensions of leadership and its potential for positive influence. Several consequences arise from this conflation:

- Limited Perspectives: The conflation of power with leadership narrows the understanding of leadership to a hierarchical and directive approach, where leaders primarily use power to exert control and influence over others. This restricts the exploration of alternative leadership styles, such as collaborative, servant, or transformational leadership, which emphasize empowerment, shared decision-making, and fostering growth among followers.
- Negative Connotations: Power is often associated with negative connotations, such as coercion, manipulation, and dominance. When power is equated with leadership, it perpetuates the belief that leadership inherently involves the use of power for self-interest or the control of others. This can undermine trust and hinder the development of positive leadership practices that prioritize ethical conduct, authenticity, and the well-being of individuals and communities.
- Exclusionary Practices: By conflating power with leadership, attention is often centered on those in formal positions of authority or designated leadership roles. This disregards the potential for leadership to emerge from various sources and individuals within a group or organization. It excludes and marginalizes those who may possess leadership qualities and capabilities but do not hold formal titles or positions of power.
- Inequality and Inequity: The conflation of power with leadership can reinforce existing power structures and exacerbate social inequalities. It maintains and reinforces hierarchical systems where power is concentrated in the hands of a few, limiting opportunities for diverse voices and perspectives to be heard and influencing decision-making processes. This perpetuates inequities and hampers efforts to create inclusive and equitable environments.

To address these challenges, it is essential to disentangle power from leadership, recognizing the multifaceted nature of leadership and its potential to inspire, empower, and positively influence others.

Within organizations, power can manifest in two primary forms: position power and personal power (Northouse, 2021). Position power is derived from an individual's specific role or rank within the formal structure of the organization. Those holding positions such as superintendents or principals wield greater power compared to staff members like teachers or paraprofessionals due to their hierarchical standing. On the other hand, personal power is derived from the influence a leader has over their followers. When leaders exhibit behaviors that hold significance for their followers, they gain power. For instance, some teachers hold power because their colleagues perceive them as admirable role models, while others possess power because folks regard them as highly skilled or considerate. In both scenarios, these leaders acquire power through how they are perceived within their relationships with others.

In education, as in many other domains, power structures play a significant role in shaping outcomes and opportunities. As educational leaders, it is crucial to gain a deeper understanding of these structures to effectively address equity issues and foster improvement. Power structures refer to the systems and hierarchies that govern how decisions are made, resources are allocated, and influence is distributed within an organization or society (Foucault, 1977). In Western society, these power structures have been predominantly shaped by those who hold the most power—White, straight men.

Tema Okun (2020) developed a framework—White supremacy culture—to describe and explain the features of power structures created by, and for the benefit of, White, straight men. White supremacy culture refers to the dominant social, political, and cultural structures and beliefs that prioritize and value Whiteness. Traditional power structures within White supremacy culture often reinforce and uphold existing systems of privilege, leading to inequitable outcomes for marginalized students. These power structures can be understood through the lens of institutional racism, which encompasses both overt and covert forms of discrimination and oppression.

Power within White supremacy culture operates through a system of dominance and privilege that perpetuates inequitable outcomes for marginalized students in schools. This system is deeply rooted in historical and societal structures that have been established and maintained through centuries of colonialism, racism, and oppression. Understanding the historical context of these power structures is crucial in comprehending their impact on educational inequities. Marginalized and disenfranchised groups, including individuals from poverty, people of color, and women, have historically borne the brunt of the impact of power structures (hooks, 1984). Power structures have often infantilized and dismissed their valid complaints, blaming them for their own status rather than recognizing the systemic barriers they face. By rationalizing their own power over others, those in positions of authority further perpetuate inequality and impede the pursuit of equity in education.

To dismantle traditional power structures and advance improvement for equity, it is crucial to recognize that knowledge about how a system works and how to improve it is not solely confined to one part of the system. Instead, it is distributed throughout the organization, with valuable insights coming from various stakeholders (Senge, 1990). By acknowledging the limitations of top-down decision-making and embracing a more inclusive approach, educational leaders can harness the collective wisdom and expertise of their entire community.

RATIONALIZATION OF POWER

In our journey to dismantle traditional power structures, it is crucial that we critically examine how power operates and rationalizes its own existence. As educational leaders, we value the importance of confronting the biases and assumptions embedded within these power structures and recognizing the ways in which they perpetuate inequities. In this section, we will delve into the rationalization of power, exploring how it influences the perception of rightness, infantilizes marginalized groups, and assigns blame. By shedding light on these mechanisms, we can begin to challenge the status quo and pave the way for transformative change.

Within traditional power structures, individuals who hold significant power often rationalize and justify their authority over others. This can occur through various mechanisms and processes that help maintain and reinforce their power position. Two common methods of rationalizing power are through ideological legitimization and institutionalization.

Ideological legitimization involves creating and promoting ideologies or belief systems that justify the existing power dynamics. This can include narratives, values, or norms that portray the powerful as deserving or superior. For example, in education, the ideology of meritocracy may be employed to justify the power and wealth of successful school or district leaders by attributing their success to individual talent and hard work (Coates, 2020). Institutionalization refers to the embedding of power structures within formal organizational or societal systems. Through the establishment of rules, regulations, and organizational practices, power is legitimized and maintained. These structures can include hierarchies, formal authority systems, and decision-making processes that concentrate power in the hands of a few individuals or positions (DiMaggio & Powell, 1983).

Educational institutions often serve as examples of rationalized power structures. Within schools, administrators, teachers, and staff hold significant power over students. This power can be rationalized through various means, such as the authority derived from their positions or expertise, the establishment of disciplinary rules and regulations, and the promotion of educational ideologies that emphasize compliance and obedience.

POWER AND THE PERCEPTION OF RIGHTNESS

The rationalization of power can sometimes lead to its misuse when those in authority start justifying and reinforcing their control. This can be a problem because those with power often believe their ideas and decisions are always right due to their ability to enforce them. This can be especially concerning in education, where it can create unequal power dynamics and hinder progress toward fairness. As educational leaders, we need to question this belief and understand that power doesn't mean infallibility. By acknowledging this, we can make room for diverse voices and perspectives.

We've all heard the snide remarks made as people transition into leadership positions: "She let the power go to her head" or "He's acting like a know-it-all." These comments stem from our collective experiences of dealing with leaders who are unable to embrace their own fallibility. In these cases, the leader's perceived self-efficacy is so high, it doesn't occur to them that they may be incorrect. Because power is viewed as the capacity or potential to influence, then rightness can be determined by a leader's ability to persuade others. Foucault explores the relationship between power, perception of rightness, rationalization, and the intertwining of power and truth in his philosophical analysis. He critiques the rationalization of power and highlights how power dynamics shape people's perception of what is considered "right" or "normal" in society. In other words, our perceptions of what is correct and what is incorrect are shaped by who is talking and our assumptions on how much power we presume they hold. Foucault argues that power not only operates through overt repression but also through the production and dissemination of knowledge, discourses, and social norms. He contends that power produces knowledge, and, in turn, knowledge reinforces and sustains power structures (Foucault, 1980).

Recently, we facilitated a session on equity-focused leadership and governance for members of a local board of education. In the discussion that followed a card sorting activity in which the participants had to match equity terms with their definitions, a White board member shared her concern with the term microaggression. After questioning whether or not microaggressions were actually a thing and dismissing the lived experiences of marginalized people, she shared her real issue with the word: "I don't understand how they can just make up a word and we are all expected to agree that it's happening." While her comment is problematic for many reasons, it is a great example of how power and rightness or truth are related. Although the term "microaggressions" was coined in the 1970s by psychiatrist and Harvard University professor Dr. Chester M. Pierce, she thought that it was a neologism coined by "woke" folks on the left. In her opinion, they don't have the power to create new terms that she has to use or be held accountable for.

This example speaks to the relationship between power and knowledge and the relationship between power and truth. Power not only produces knowledge but also determines what counts as truth within a given society. Truth is not an absolute or objective entity but is shaped by power relations. Power operates through systems of knowledge, discourses, and institutions that define and regulate what is considered true or false, normal or abnormal.

Traditional power structures in schools can perpetuate what Foucault calls truth regimes that privilege certain voices and perspectives while marginalizing others. A truth regime refers to the dominant system of knowledge and discourse that defines what is considered true or valid within a particular society or historical period. Truth regimes are frameworks through which knowledge is produced, organized, and regulated, shaping what is accepted as truth and what is considered false or deviant. They not only reinforce existing power dynamics but also influence individuals' perceptions of what is considered "right" or "normal."

Truth regimes are not objective or neutral but are intimately tied to power relations and serve to uphold existing power structures. They operate through various institutions, discourses, and practices that establish and enforce what is considered valid knowledge, acceptable behavior, and normative standards. In the context of education, standardized testing creates a truth regime by establishing a set of predetermined knowledge and skills that students are expected to possess. This truth regime shapes the curriculum, teaching methods, and even the way students perceive and understand knowledge.

The consequence of such a truth regime is that it marginalizes alternative perspectives and reinforces existing power hierarchies. Students, teachers, and other stakeholders may feel silenced or dismissed if their views do not align with the dominant discourse, perpetuating a cycle where power reproduces itself through the production and dissemination of knowledge.

INFANTILIZATION AND BLAME

As educational leaders, we have often failed to unpack the rationalization of power and recognize the truth regimes that we exist in and how they stand in opposition to the lived experiences of all stakeholders. As a result, it becomes easy to adopt a paternalistic or authoritarian stance, where the leaders perceive themselves as having all the knowledge and expertise and those they lead are seen as passive recipients of knowledge. One particularly insidious manifestation of power rationalization is the infantilization of marginalized groups where those in power dismiss the concerns and experiences of individuals from poverty, people of color, and women by treating them as less capable or less deserving of respect. This form of condescension not only perpetuates inequity but also reinforces power imbalances.

Patronizing or condescending treatment of individuals or groups from marginalized communities undermines their autonomy, agency, and intellectual capabilities. In education, marginalized individuals—students and adults—are often treated as children who require constant guidance and supervision, rather than as equals with their own knowledge and experiences. We have watched this play out in the disproportionate use of disciplinary measures against BIPOC students. Research has shown that BIPOC students are more likely to receive harsher punishments compared to their White peers for similar behaviors (Skiba et al., 2011).

Recently we facilitated focus groups with high school students who shared how infantilization plays out in the classroom. Students reported that many of their teachers seem hyperfocused on the actions of BIPOC students and react to even the slightest off-task behaviors. This discriminatory treatment perpetuates the perception that BIPOC students are incapable of self-regulation and require constant discipline and control.

So why is infantilizing a bad idea? If we believe marginalized folks don't know what's best for them, we will never engage and equip them as agents of their own liberation, as emphasized by Paulo Freire (1970). Freire believed that individuals, regardless of their marginalized status, possess the capacity to critically reflect on their own reality, challenge oppressive structures, and actively engage in the process of liberation. Freire argued that the process of liberation is a transformative journey that requires the active participation and agency of the oppressed.

Infantilization is only one by-product of traditional power structures. While infantilization is on one end of the spectrum, characterized by the patriarchal belief that you have no idea how to get out of this predicament, blame—your predicament is all your fault—sits at the other end. The blame game is frequently employed as a means of rationalizing and maintaining power differentials. People in positions of power often shift responsibility onto those who are marginalized, suggesting that their status is a result of their own deficiencies or choices. In the process of identifying areas of improvement in service of equity, marginalized individuals are often scapegoated, held responsible for their own circumstances as a way to absolve those in power from any responsibility.

Our first example of the blame game is reflected in the ways in which educators have worked to close the achievement gap. Rather than examining systemic inequities that contribute to this gap, educators have attributed it to the students' supposed lack of effort or motivation. While we have learned that it's problematic to openly blame marginalized students for the persistent gaps in achievement outcomes, our beliefs about who or what is at fault surface in our interventions. When we believe that students are to blame for the gaps, we employ interventions that are designed to fix students. When we blame the structural inequalities and systemic barriers that preclude all students from achieving at high levels, we work on fixing the system.

Our second example is related to professional advancement. Women and educators of color often face barriers when seeking professional advancement opportunities. In some instances, they may be blamed for not being assertive or proactive enough in pursuing career growth, rather than recognizing the systemic biases that limit their progress. This blame further marginalizes and undermines the experiences and qualifications of these educators and conveniently deflects attention away from the systemic barriers and biases that contribute to inequity in the first place.

INTERROGATING THE STATUS QUO

As the school bell chimed, signaling the start of another day, Principal Thompson, an instructional leader renowned for her unwavering dedication to her staff, walked down the hallways. Although her desire to improve outcomes for all students is closely aligned with the district priorities, she often found herself at odds with the system's entrenched practices. Though she encouraged her teachers to challenge the status quo, she couldn't help but notice the subtle pressure emanating from the central office—an undercurrent that inadvertently nudged educators back to the familiar, well-trodden path, disregarding the needs of marginalized students.

The status quo, defined as the existing state of affairs or the prevailing social order, often operates as an unexamined foundation within educational systems. It encompasses a web of beliefs, practices, and power dynamics that unknowingly reinforce and uphold inequitable structures. Within schools, the status quo can be observed in standardized curricula that prioritize Eurocentric perspectives and marginalize diverse forms of knowledge or the disciplinary practices that disproportionately target and punish students from marginalized communities, perpetuating cycles of oppression. The status quo also shows up in the perpetuation of homogenous leadership structures that exclude marginalized voices from decision-making processes. Maintaining the status quo stands in stark opposition to a liberatory approach to equity improvement. By uncritically accepting and perpetuating the existing power structures, educational institutions inadvertently perpetuate social hierarchies and inhibit progress toward equity. The status quo shields itself from scrutiny by presenting itself as "normal," "natural," or "neutral."

In Chapter 1, we highlighted the importance of being hard on systems and soft on people. In our work with leaders, we have witnessed principals' frustration with teachers who are "stuck in their ways" or are "unwilling to change" despite their recognition of the disparate outcomes experienced by marginalized students. But what if we told ourselves a different story to explain people's inherent desire to maintain the status quo, even when it's not working for them?

We believe that educators' inclination to maintain the status quo does not necessarily stem from a lack of belief in equity or a desire for exceptional outcomes for all students. Instead, we recognize how the status quo is deeply intertwined with our inherent human tendency toward homeostasis—the natural inclination to seek stability, balance, and equilibrium in our surroundings. Recognizing this aspect of human nature can help us understand why even well-intentioned educators may find themselves resistant to change and inadvertently perpetuating the existing system.

Research in psychology and sociology sheds light on the powerful influence of homeostasis on human behavior. Social psychologist Leon Festinger introduced the concept of cognitive dissonance (Festinger, 1957), which explains that individuals experience discomfort when their beliefs or actions conflict with one another. This discomfort motivates individuals to reduce the dissonance and restore equilibrium by aligning their beliefs and behaviors with the existing status quo. In the context of education, this means that when educators are confronted with initiatives that challenge the established norms and practices, a natural inclination to maintain equilibrium arises. Acknowledging this pull of homeostasis helps us to be softer on people and harder on the system by exploring change ideas that are designed to overcome the gravitational force of the status quo.

Interrogating the status quo goes beyond the application of an equity lens to analyze systemic inequities. It requires leaders to engage in mirror work—critically reflecting on their own biases, reactions, and investment in maintaining the existing system. This process of self-exploration is paramount to fostering true transformation and promoting authentic change because it helps us understand how we unwittingly contribute to the maintenance of the status quo. This introspective process requires leaders to critically reflect on their responses when confronted by teachers, students, and parents who push back on their ideas, particularly when those ideas merely represent a polished version of the existing system.

RENEGOTIATING POWER

In a bustling school district, Principal Ramirez was known for her passion for equity and her desire to improve outcomes for marginalized students. Publicly, she espoused the importance of listening and engaging all stakeholders—especially those representing marginalized identities within the school's community. However, behind closed doors, her beliefs about power as a limited resource and her perception of power sharing as a zero-sum game hindered her ability to fully engage in the work of interrogating and renegotiating power. This mindset inadvertently impeded her focus on equity improvement and perpetuated the existing power dynamics within her school.

When it came to decision-making processes, Principal Ramirez was accustomed to having the final say. She believed that maintaining control over power was crucial for maintaining order and ensuring accountability. She saw power as something finite, and any relinquishment of power to teachers, students, or parents would diminish her authority and influence. This underlying belief limited her willingness to genuinely distribute power and engage in collaborative decision-making processes that would amplify marginalized voices and perspectives.

As the school embarked on an equity-focused initiative, Principal Ramirez found herself defaulting back to her familiar top-down approach. While she recognized the importance of involving teachers, students, and parents in decision-making, her deep-rooted belief that power sharing equated to power loss made her hesitant to fully embrace their contributions. She inadvertently overlooked the expertise and experiences of those at the margins, inadvertently perpetuating a system where power remained concentrated in her hands and reinforcing the status quo.

This is a good place to stop and acknowledge that this type of liberatory leadership is hard. We all know a version of Principal Ramirez. Perhaps you are a Principal Ramirez. A genuine focus on equity improvement necessitates a fundamental renegotiation of power dynamics within the educational system. As leaders, our willingness to redistribute power is influenced by our beliefs about power itself. If we perceive power as a limited resource and view power sharing as a zero-sum game where our own power diminishes with each instance of sharing, we may be reluctant to engage fully in the critical work of redistributing power. Conversely, if we understand power sharing as akin to sharing knowledge—where sharing does not diminish our own understanding but rather enhances it—we are more likely to embrace the idea of redistributing power and empowering those at the margins to become agents of their own liberation.

By dismantling traditional power structures, educational leaders can create space for the redistribution of power and acknowledge the expertise and knowledge that exists throughout the system. This recognition requires a reimagining of leadership as a collective endeavor, where decision-making processes are inclusive, participatory, and driven by shared goals of equity and improvement. It involves engaging teachers, students, parents, and community members as active partners in shaping policies, practices, and initiatives.

Moreover, embracing distributed expertise challenges the notion that knowledge resides solely within hierarchical positions of authority. Cultivating a culture of shared power and distributed expertise requires ongoing dialogue, collaboration, and reflection. It necessitates the creation of spaces for authentic engagement, where individuals can challenge existing power dynamics, voice their concerns, and contribute to decision-making processes.

EMBRACING TRANSFORMATIVE CHANGE

As leaders, we often find ourselves grappling with the profound responsibility of addressing equity concerns in our schools amidst this deep-seated desire to default back to the status quo. We strive to create an educational landscape that uplifts and empowers marginalized students, dismantling the barriers that hinder their success. While our intention to embrace equity-focused initiatives is commendable, it is crucial to recognize that many of these endeavors lack the depth necessary for true transformation. Instead, they often fall prey to becoming cosmetic alterations, merely polishing the existing status quo without addressing its fundamental shortcomings.

The allure of these well-intentioned initiatives is undeniable. With promises of improved outcomes, heightened inclusivity, and narrowed achievement gaps, they appear to be the key to fostering a fair and just educational environment. Yet we must be cautious not to fall victim to the illusion they create, as their underlying structure and implementation may inadvertently reinforce the very systems we seek to challenge.

One of the main pitfalls lies in the tendency to adopt a surface-level approach to equity. Many initiatives, driven by external pressures or mandated directives, focus on surface-level changes rather than delving deep into the systemic issues that perpetuate educational inequities. Superficial alterations such as diversity training workshops, cultural sensitivity programs, or inclusive curriculum additions, while valuable in their own right, often fail to address the systemic biases deeply embedded in the educational fabric.

Moreover, these initiatives can unwittingly perpetuate a sense of complacency among educators. By providing a veneer of progress without addressing the underlying power structures, they create an illusion that the system is evolving, when in reality, it remains largely unchanged. This false sense of transformation can lull educational leaders and teachers into a state of comfort, where they believe they are making a difference without challenging the very foundations that uphold educational disparities.

Additionally, the lack of adequate support and resources allocated to these initiatives hinders their potential for meaningful impact. When equity-focused endeavors are launched without the necessary investment in professional development, time for collaboration, and allocation of resources, they often become mere checkmarks on a to-do list. Teachers and administrators, burdened with existing responsibilities, struggle to fully engage with these initiatives, limiting their efficacy and perpetuating the superficial nature of the intended change.

To truly transform our educational landscape and uplift marginalized students, we must move beyond the superficiality of these well-intentioned yet insufficient initiatives. We must confront the uncomfortable truths that underpin the status quo and challenge the existing power structures that perpetuate inequities. This requires a paradigm shift in our approach—one that prioritizes authentic engagement, systemic change, and a commitment to addressing the root causes of educational disparities.

TIME AS A TOOL OF POWER

As we delve deeper into the intricate web of power and equity, we encounter a dimension that often remains unseen but profoundly shapes the course of human interactions and societal structures—time. Just as power operates as a force that influences relationships, decision-making, and resource distribution, the notion of time wields its influence over the narratives we construct, the histories we remember, and the urgency we assign to transformative endeavors. In this section, we embark on a journey through the temporal dimension, uncovering how time interweaves with power dynamics and the pursuit of equity.

Time, often seen as a neutral and unchanging constant, can be wielded as a tool of power to shape perceptions, reinforce hierarchies, and perpetuate inequities. Controlling the narratives about history, the passage of time, and the linear progression of societal norms can be employed strategically by those in positions of authority. These narratives serve to legitimize and maintain existing power structures. By framing historical events selectively and dictating which stories are preserved, those in power can manipulate collective memory and consciousness. This selective control over historical memory not only influences how societies perceive different groups' capabilities and worth but also sustains the power imbalances that have evolved over time.

The intricate relationship between time, patience, and urgency presents a delicate balance in the pursuit of equity. Navigating this balance is essential for meaningful and sustainable change. The urgency to address systemic inequities is undeniable, driven by the recognition of the ongoing harm inflicted on marginalized communities. Yet an overemphasis on immediate results can inadvertently perpetuate existing power dynamics. Superficial changes that prioritize short-term outcomes may fail to address the underlying structures that maintain inequities.

Simultaneously, an overly impatient approach risks undermining the transformative potential of equity work. Meaningful change often requires time to dismantle deeply ingrained systems and beliefs. Root causes of inequity are complex and multifaceted, necessitating a long-term commitment to systemic change. Patience becomes a powerful ally in this process, allowing space for comprehensive analyses, critical reflections, and the cultivation of authentic collaborations.

Balancing urgency with patience, however, is not a call for complacency. It is an acknowledgment of the need for strategic and deliberate actions that challenge the root causes of inequity while fostering environments that encourage long-term engagement. The process of transformation is gradual and requires sustained effort, collaboration, and a shared commitment to dismantling oppressive structures over time.

As we explore the relationship between time, power, and equity, it becomes evident that a nuanced and time-conscious approach is crucial. Recognizing the interconnectedness of these elements allows us to navigate the complexities of the temporal dimension with intentionality and purpose, ensuring that our efforts to disrupt power imbalances and advance equity are both effective and sustainable.

LIBERATORY POWER SHARING

"For the master's tools will never dismantle the master's house. They may allow us to temporarily beat him at his own game, but they will never enable us to bring about genuine change."

—Audre Lorde, 1984, p. 122

We recently had the opportunity to present at the annual Carnegie Summit. While the goal of our session was similar to the mission of this book—to get people thinking about the intersection of equity and improvement science— we also wanted the participants to experience an intentional shift in power dynamics. As people continued to file into the room, we announced that we would engage folks in a series of discussions related to demystifying, decolonizing, and democratizing improvement science in service of equity. After reviewing the quote earlier, we invited folks to get into small groups of four or five to discuss what they believed Lorde meant by the master's tools. Typically, we would've begun this discussion with introductions—share your name, where you're from, and what you do. Instead, we instructed the participants to only share their names with their group members.

This simple facilitation move was one of several strategies we used to create a holding environment that pushed against White supremacy norms, and we modeled it from the start. We introduced ourselves as Isobel and

Rydell from Connecticut and told them that was all they needed to know about us in order to dive into the discussion. Before they had the time to google us, we got them up and working in groups. By disallowing folks to talk about their rank and title, we disrupted the power dynamics that are naturally associated with people's positions and challenged the White supremacy norm of basing the quality of an individual's contribution on their qualifications.

What resulted from this simple shift was astounding. In addition to receiving positive feedback on the substance of the session and the opportunity to share ideas and learn from others, participants shared that their ability to engage authentically with others during the session felt easier because they weren't tied to the baggage that is attached to their titles and roles. In other words, they were able to dig deeper into the discussion because there was no energy wasted in trying to prove yourself. Hours after the session, a participant named Sonya caught up with us and expressed her appreciation. She introduced herself as a former performing arts teacher who is now supporting districts in their improvement science efforts related to reading. Sonya talked about the difficulties she has experienced working with leaders who, despite her improvement experience and formal studies, question her ability because she didn't teach a core subject. For Sonya, the Carnegie session was the first meaningful discussion she's had with other leaders where she wasn't distracted by her perceived lack of qualifications or the power hoarding from those who saw themselves as more qualified. Without prompting, she shared that her discussion group had identified power hoarding as one of the master's tools and recognized that creating a power paradigm is an essential tool needed to dismantle the house.

Audre Lorde's (1984) metaphor of dismantling the master's house and the master's tools offers a profound perspective on the transformative potential of challenging and dismantling oppressive systems within the educational context. As we embark on the journey of dismantling traditional power structures, we must acknowledge that true transformation requires us to reevaluate the very foundations on which our educational systems are built. In Lorde's metaphor, the master's house represents the existing structures of power and privilege that perpetuate oppression and inequality. These structures are sustained by the tools that have been historically employed to maintain dominance and control over marginalized groups. By relying solely on these tools, we inadvertently reinforce the very systems we seek to dismantle.

So, what exactly are the master's tools? We believe the master's house is White supremacy culture—the dominant social, political, and cultural systems that prioritize and perpetuate the interests of White individuals or groups over those of marginalized communities. Therefore, the master's tools are the intentional or unintentional ways in which we uphold and perpetuate the White supremacy cultural characteristics identified in Okun's work. One of these characteristics, power hoarding, plays a significant role in maintaining the status quo and perpetuating inequities. Power hoarding manifests in schools through the consolidation of decision-making authority and control within a select few individuals or groups. This power dynamic operates on multiple levels, from individual classrooms to entire school districts. Consequently, the voices and experiences of these individuals are often silenced or overshadowed, further perpetuating the marginalization and disenfranchisement they face.

What is the antidote to power hoarding? Power sharing? While we view power sharing or distributive leadership—emphasizing collaboration, shared decision-making, and the involvement of multiple stakeholders—as a step in the right direction, we believe it is important to explore how power is shared and with whom and uncover the underlying motivation for inviting others to the leadership table.

It should be no surprise that we advocate for sharing power with teachers, students, and their families—specifically those with firsthand experiences at the margins. But we don't think that they should just be at the decision-making table to offer feedback on plans that are already developed. We believe authentic liberatory power sharing ensures those without institutional power are included in both the development and creation of the plan and the identification and unpacking of the problem that necessitates an improvement plan. Often, even with a focus on distributed leadership, leaders are seen as the strategists who develop plans for improvement, and subordinates become the tacticians who follow orders and implement said plan with fidelity. In this model, sharing power means giving (qualified) tacticians a chance to offer their feedback and making tweaks to the plan based on their thoughts. While this is a huge step up from infantilizing teachers, it assumes that those in power have identified the correct issues to address and have a full understanding of the problem and the system that produces it. Further, it assumes that the best solutions lie in the hands of those in power.

This type of transactional power sharing where people are empowered (for a finite amount of time) to assist in the refinement of plans and/or strategies developed by leaders falls short of dismantling traditional power structures. Transactional power sharing is simply an improved version of power hoarding, making it one of the master's tools that we should avoid. Transactional power sharing positions leaders as designers or architects and subordinates as implementers and builders. Often, this transactional power-sharing approach is employed as a response to the central office's mandate to engage a diverse group of stakeholders in the improvement process. The result of this performative approach to sharing power is the dissolution of trust from underrepresented stakeholder groups who were excited to be fully engaged in the work of improvement.

Over the years, we have sat in countless interviews where candidates reference Spillane's work on distributive leadership to describe how they view leading as a collective and collaborative process. When probed to elaborate, candidates typically share stories of how they have included teachers and families in their decision-making process. Occasionally, candidates proudly talk about how they even empowered students to be a part of the process. In most cases, candidates' views of distributed leadership and sharing power are simply a matter of delegating tasks or responsibilities, including additional stakeholders in the planning and/or implementation process, and engaging in transactional power sharing focused on increasing buy-in (Gronn, 2002).

As principals, we took pride in positioning ourselves as distributive leaders. Faced with the common view of power as a means of dominating others or exercising control over them, we wanted to align ourselves with Mary Parker Follett's view of power as a positive and constructive force that arises from within relationships and groups (Metcalf & Urwick, 2003). Follett—a pioneering management theorist and social philosopher who advocated for a more democratic and participatory approach to power in organizations and society—rejected the traditional hierarchical and coercive notions of power (power-over) in favor of a more inclusive and participatory approach that emphasizes collaboration, integration, and shared responsibility (power-with and power-to).

Power-over refers to the traditional understanding of power as domination and control. It is a hierarchical form of power where one person or group exercises authority over others, often through coercion or force. Power-over is based on the ability to impose one's will on others and make them comply through fear or punishment. Power-with is a more cooperative and participatory form of power. It emerges from the integration of diverse perspectives and interests within a group or organization. Power-with recognizes that individuals have different expertise, experiences, and viewpoints, and it seeks to harness the collective wisdom and resources of a group. It involves collaborative decision-making, shared responsibility, and a focus on finding mutually beneficial solutions. Power-with emphasizes the importance of building relationships, fostering open communication, and facilitating cooperation among people. Finally, power-to refers to the capacity or potential for action and change. It is the ability to bring about desired outcomes, overcome obstacles, and create positive change in oneself and the world. Power-to is not limited to a single person or position but is distributed among individuals and groups within a social system. It involves recognizing and developing one's own capabilities and supporting others in realizing their potential for action and influence.

Most of the leaders we've encountered promote the idea of power-with and believe in the power of distributed leadership, recognizing that leadership is not limited to a single person or position but can be exercised by multiple individuals at different levels (Spillane, 2006). For them, the primary goal of sharing power is to improve organizational effectiveness and enhance collective decision-making and problem solving. While we see this as a noble goal, we are more interested in liberatory power sharing that builds on the transformational potential of power-to, which enables individuals to have agency, influence, and the ability to make meaningful choices, thereby fostering a sense of empowerment.

Liberatory power sharing can be defined as the transformative and equitable distribution of power within a social or institutional context, aimed at dismantling oppressive systems and structures and empowering marginalized individuals and communities. It involves challenging and disrupting hierarchies, biases, and systems of domination, while centering the voices, agency, and self-determination of those who have historically been marginalized. Liberatory power sharing goes beyond the distribution of leadership roles and highlights the transformative and equitable use of power, particularly in the context of marginalized individuals and communities. While distributed leadership may still operate within existing power structures, liberatory power sharing challenges and seeks to dismantle oppressive systems and hierarchies. It aims to disrupt and transform power dynamics by centering the agency and self-determination of marginalized individuals and communities, working toward social justice and liberation.

Liberatory power explicitly acknowledges historical and structural inequities, focusing on the empowerment of marginalized groups as a means of challenging and dismantling systems of oppression. It emphasizes the inclusion of diverse perspectives, the recognition of different forms of knowledge, and the intentional engagement of those who have been marginalized. Liberatory power seeks to create conditions for social transformation and to address systemic inequities, while distributed leadership primarily aims to improve organizational functioning.

So, how can we operationalize this notion of liberatory power sharing as we work to improve outcomes for all students? To answer this question, we turn to improvement science—specifically liberatory improvement science, which provides a robust framework that emphasizes the importance of power being shared, decentralized, and used in ways that promote justice, equity, and liberation. In improvement science, improvement teams are collaborative groups of individuals who come together to work on specific improvement initiatives. These teams typically consist of diverse stakeholders, such as teachers, administrators, students, parents, and community members, who collectively analyze data, develop strategies, implement changes, and monitor progress to address identified challenges or achieve desired outcomes. In liberatory improvement science, improvement teams intentionally include those who have historically been marginalized or underrepresented as well as those who are located closest to the problem. In most cases, this means having students actively engaged as members of the improvement team. This intentional inclusion acknowledges and values the expertise, perspectives, and experiences of all team members, ensuring that power is shared and decision-making is distributed more equitably. Additionally, this intentional inclusion requires those with positional power to listen aggressively, suspend certainty, and take up less discussion space as the team works to identify the problem, interrogate the system that produces the problem, and generate ideas for change that may lead to improvement.

AT YOUR DESK OR IN THE HALLS

Although improvement science is rooted in collaboration, it remains agnostic when it comes to dismantling traditional power structures. In other words, a school can engage in the improvement science process and share power by engaging diverse stakeholders but never work to dismantle traditional power structures. But engaging in equity-focused work aimed at improving outcomes for marginalized students without working to dismantle the very power structures that have led to the outcomes you are trying to improve is futile. Moreover, it runs the risk of inflicting even more harm on the most vulnerable populations by inviting marginalized folks to the leadership table and then engaging them in transactional power sharing that discounts their funds of knowledge and lessons learned from their lived experiences.

Liberatory improvement science, however, strives for the redistribution of power, recognizing that those most affected by the challenges should be agents in the problem solving and decision-making process. By empowering marginalized individuals to participate in designing and implementing improvements, improvement teams affirm their expertise and enable them to drive change that reflects their unique needs and aspirations. In liberatory improvement science, liberatory power sharing is not only a transactional means to yielding better outcomes. It is about exemplifying an adjacent possible reality in which the redistribution of power leads to increased agency among marginalized folks. Further, liberatory improvement science seeks to challenge and transform oppressive structures as its goal while simultaneously enabling individuals and communities to shape their own destinies and create more just and equitable societies throughout the process.

If power is defined as the ability or capacity to influence others, make decisions, and shape the direction of an organization, then sharing power and empowering others require more than offering opportunities for feedback. Just because we are writing this book doesn't mean that we have not fallen into the trap of transactional power sharing.

Following are a few reflection questions we use to determine our willingness to actually share power with those who have been empowered to engage in the improvement process. These questions go beyond determining whether or not power was shared. Instead, they ask about how power was shared.

Reflection Questions

- Who is influencing whom? Is my sharing power really about getting stakeholder "buy-in" and influencing others to get on board? Have I allowed myself to be influenced by those I've empowered, or do I see influence as a one-way street?
- Who is making decisions? Am I willing to let others make decisions? Do all opinions and insights hold the same weight, or is it determined by title?
- Who is shaping the direction of the organization? Is setting the vision and/or determining the focus of our improvement efforts my responsibility as the leader?
- How do I share power with stakeholders who have historically been marginalized? What strategies do I use to solicit their input and engage them in the improvement processes?
- How do I rationalize my own power?

CHAPTER 7

Broadening Our Concept of Data

It is very likely that equity advocates have witnessed data—or more accurately, a narrow conceptualization of data—being used to explain or justify policies and practices that have harmed marginalized students; as in all things, there is no such thing as equity neutral, and data that are not being used to improve experiences and outcomes for marginalized students are reinforcing a racist status quo. The implication of data in the further marginalization of marginalized students has led some equity advocates to argue for the elimination of standardized testing, grades, and other sources of data and to some hostility toward improvement science (Safir & Dugan, 2021).

The testing hiatus brought about by the pandemic was an opportunity to call out a deficit-driven ideology in the design of standardized tests and to call for the dismantling of the entire apparatus. This is an easy argument to make: Standardized testing of students takes up precious instructional time; a focus on the "basics" constricts the taught curriculum, reducing children's exposure to a breadth of ideas and activities during school; testing disadvantages large groups of students and drives deficit thinking and low expectations; and testing tied to consequences exposes how the system works but makes the mistake of placing responsibility in the wrong place and on the wrong people.

And yet, how will you know that there has been any improvement without collecting data? How will you know that the system has not become worse instead of better? Data are essential for monitoring progress. You don't have to be a proponent of current accountability policies to see data as an essential part of education reform. Much as we may dislike the unintended consequences created by the current system, it is difficult to change a system that you can't even see. Without the transparency afforded by data, it is impossible to know if marginalized students continue to be victims of low expectations, lower funding, and other features of systems that discriminate against them (Johnson and LaSalle, 2010).

Educators may not be ignorant of data policies and practices that have negatively impacted students, yet still not understand why data can be such a trigger for equity advocates. This chapter, therefore, addresses thinking about data in service of equity, which may represent a significant shift in approach for everyone involved: equity advocates who have learned to be cynical and skeptical when it comes to the use of data; school leaders who have learned that the only data that matter are numbers, percentages, and outcomes; and improvers who want to use data well in their pursuit of equity. So, we start this chapter with a short history of the abuse of data and the use of data to abuse.

DATA CONTAMINATED BY HISTORY

When Russia started its large-scale invasion of Ukraine in February 2022, American and European journalists reported how stunning it was to see fighting in "civilized" countries, saying things like, "These are prosperous, middle-class people. These are not people trying to get away from areas in North Africa. They look like any European family that you would live next door to" (Carras, 2022). Apart from the fact that they seemed to have forgotten what they surely knew about genocide during the Holocaust, and even more recently in the Balkans, they were displaying a mental model of the world divided into civilized and uncivilized along racial lines—it's shocking to see a White city bombed, it's shocking to see White refugees, it's shocking to see people who "look like us" being dragged into conflict. Trevor Noah, on *The Daily Show* (February 28, 2022), called out this reporting, saying, "I don't know about you, but I was shocked to see how many reporters, around the world, by the way, seem to think that it's more of a tragedy when White people have to flee their countries."

We are confident that these journalists would deny that they are racist—and we believe them, in the sense that they hold an explicit belief, in line with their sense of themselves as good and decent human beings, in equality and would never intentionally discriminate against a person of color or use a racial epithet (Bonilla-Silva, 2021). What their language betrays is an unexamined but widely shared mental model of what it means to be civilized, and therefore superior, that attaches to people who look a certain way and, ipso facto, does not attach to people who do not possess those visible features. This mental model is widespread, ingrained, and goes a long way to explaining the mistrust that people of color have for the use of data to make decisions about children.

There is a long history of the use of data to "prove" White superiority. There are several excellent histories of how the skin color, facial features, and even hair type of the people we typically think of as White became conflated with the concept of race and racial superiority and how White scientists and mathematicians embarked on a mission using science, which was of course presumed to be neutral and unbiased, to prove that Whites were the superior race and therefore both entitled to their positions of power and to subjugate persons of other races (Saini, 2019). Nell Irvin Painter

(2010), in *A History of White People*, describes the development of a concept of race to justify slavery, racism, colonialism, and subjugation. In *The Mismeasure of Man*, Stephen Jay Gould (1996) described how White male scientists intentionally selected data to support the logic of their argument of the superiority, particularly regarding intelligence, of people with light skin tones. (They didn't work quite so hard to prove the superiority of men over women, as that distinction was held to be obvious.) In *Thicker Than Blood*, a history of statistics to prove theories of ranking by race, Tukufu Zuberi (2001) documents the development of statistical methods by Francis Galton, cousin of Charles Darwin, to justify eugenics. Further, as Fields and Fields (2012) point out, it is much easier to believe that people are inferior by nature when they are already seen as oppressed; there is, therefore, a self-reinforcing loop where this bias, and indeed most biases, is concerned.

The faith of White male scientists in their ability to accurately sort and rank has cast a long shadow; educators' espoused beliefs about equality, equity, and the vision we have for "all students" live alongside persistent practices of ranking and sorting that reinforce patterns of marginalization and inequity. These practices are held in place by the accountability structures under which educators work, and over which they have little control. No Child Left Behind (NCLB) and Every Student Succeeds Act (ESSA) enforce attention to outcome measures that were intended to reduce variation in outcome according to race, gender, dis/ability, and home language. We think it's important to examine the logic of an education system that is so focused on certain types of results—partly so that the traps of a test-based theory of action can be avoided but also so that data that can support continuous improvement can be actively sought and acted on.

A TEST-BASED THEORY OF ACTION

In education, some forms of data are revered more than others; specifically, data in the form of numbers generated by standards-based testing drive much of the thinking around policy and planning. This feature of the field over the last 50 years results from several converging policies. First, special education law provides funding not for students who need extra help to meet standards, but for students who meet precisely defined criteria for a list of possible handicapping conditions; therefore, standardized tests are required to identify students who qualify for services. Second, NCLB and its precursors at the state level required districts to meet explicit benchmarks using standardized tests of achievement. Similarly, and in the same category, Race to the Top awarded funds to states that were willing to adopt teacher evaluation plans that included "value-add" measures of teacher effectiveness, again based on standardized tests of achievement.

Third, superintendents and principals began to be required to write strategic or school improvement plans based on Kaplan and Norton's (1996) dictum, "If you can't measure it, you can't manage it" (p. 21); this has driven school and district planning for decades, free of any nuance the authors intended. The plans that superintendents and principals are required to write typically place a heavy emphasis on meeting goals that are based on quantitative data measuring student outcomes. Frequently, this leads to the collection and analysis of data based on what is easily measured as opposed to what really matters (Beach, 2021). Fourth, testing companies built on a market already primed to see testing as a de facto part of a strategy and marketed tests for formative assessment, shifting the meaning of formative assessment away from the meaning in the research that supports the practice (Black & Wiliam, 1998b). And finally, perhaps of lesser importance but significant nonetheless, academic studies of effective educational practice rely on standardized measures of student achievement.

All this has led to a dominant mental model among teachers and leaders that the word "data" means numbers, that goals must be specified in terms of quantitative outcomes, that accountability is grounded in measurable outcomes, and that, to some degree, the ends justify the means. In our work, we frequently encounter issues based on this mental model. For example, schools are typically required to submit plans to their district central office for feedback, and more often than not the only feedback they receive is connected to their goal and whether it is attainable, on the one hand, or ambitious enough, on the other; central office leaders, therefore, appear agnostic as to the processes in place for schools to reach their outcome-based goals.

We often have to clarify our use of the word data when working with school leaders or school-based teams: that data need not be only outcome measures, and they need not be numbers at all. We have learned the hard way that we should not ask the question, "What data do you have?" without explaining first of all that we mean any evidence about the question under consideration; otherwise, we will be told that there are no data, only to find out later that actually all kinds of information are available, including student and parent interviews, classroom observations, historical patterns, and sometimes even course enrollment numbers and grades that, because they are not test-based outcomes, nobody thought to mention. Educators have a mental model that "anecdotal evidence" is inadequate, and we have to point out that what people say about their experience is the foundation of many research traditions.

As a result, equity-focused educators should be forgiven for developing a mental model of even well-intended reform that sees any effort at improvement, including improvement science, as prioritizing tools over people; idolizing quantitative results; being outcomes-driven to the exclusion of any attention to process; generating a hard-edged definition of accountability;

and displaying indifference to equity, since numbers and measurement and all kinds of "hard data" have been used for decades—even centuries—to prove the superiority of some and the inferiority of others.

A view of improvement science as indifferent to means is ironic, because Deming, to whom most improvers trace their intellectual roots, emphasized "It is wrong to suppose that if you can't measure it, you can't manage it—a costly myth" (Deming, 2018, p. 26). Deming's whole approach, which came to be known as total quality management (TQM), was based on the following principle: "A numerical goal accomplishes nothing. Only the method is important, not the goal" (p, 23). Deming emphasized that it is the system that is producing the results, and we should not ascribe to the people working within the system more power than they really have to change the results.

In other words, if a pencil factory generates only 95 pencils of acceptable quality for every 100 pencils produced and that is true no matter which worker is assigned to the production line, then there is no point in rating the workers as below proficient, because the workers are just one part of a system that generates substandard pencils. To improve the number of perfect pencils, you have to improve the system (i.e., the process for producing the pencils). Hence, the emphasis is on improving the process (to generate fewer imperfect pencils), rather than quality control (finding the imperfect pencils when they've already been produced but before they are shipped to the customer). The concept of looking at the whole system in order to improve is the reason that the practice is called TQM. As mentioned in Chapter 1, most educational leaders are familiar with the idea of systems thinking and have heard the term "every system is perfectly designed to get the results it gets," but not many are equipped to follow that edict to its logical conclusion: that they should be directing their leadership efforts at improving the process rather than basing their all of their decisions on, nor "holding people accountable" for, outcome data.

Deming's ideas, it should be emphasized, were not translated accurately into education. Site-based management, the precursor of today's emphasis on outcomes-based accountability, claimed Deming as a major influence while completely misrepresenting what he advocated. Deming despised performance evaluation, management by objective, and numerical goals, as outlined in his "14 Points" (Deming, 1982). Deming saw that the outcomes were created by the system, and therefore the way to improve outcomes—the only way—is to improve the system. But in education we veer toward holding the students rather than the system accountable. We also explain system-level issues by invoking student-level factors. Ladson-Billings (2006) has pointed out that the use of the term "achievement gap" distorts the way that patterns of achievement are conceptualized and fails to take into account the "education debt" that is owed to students who have been subject to fewer educational opportunities; lower expectations; testing that is normed on White, American, middle-class language and culture; and schools that are underresourced.

Data used in schools today often seems designed to reinforce a deficit mindset. As Senge (1990) points out, the way you see the problem is the problem—if data collection and analysis promote the view of some groups of children as underperforming relative to others, then the children themselves are too easily seen as deficient, which leads to their being treated as deficient. If, however, the measures were to shift focus to how the system produces outcomes where some students benefit and some lose out, then the system is seen as the root of the problem, and therefore the locus of potential solutions is in changing the system. Educators who have spent a career invested in working toward equity are deeply suspicious of educators who appear to see methods such as improvement science as equity-neutral. The language and logic of antiracism have pervaded the work of equity in schools, and equity-focused educators are likely to embrace ideas popularized by Ibram Kendi (2019): There is no such thing as race- or equity-neutral—rather, a policy or practice is either driving toward equity or it is reproducing the status quo, and since the status quo is inequitable, failure to disrupt the status quo is inherently racist.

POOR ASSUMPTIONS AND UNINTENDED CONSEQUENCES

"The soft bigotry of low expectations" is the most enduring phrase from the Bush-era educational reforms. The line is from a speech President Bush gave to the National Association for the Advancement of Colored People (NAACP) in 2000, before the passage of NCLB in 2001. NCLB was not Bush's first exposure to high-stakes accountability. He had been governor of Texas, where the previous Democratic administration under Governor Ann Richards sponsored a very similar system of holding districts and schools accountable for their scores on statewide standardized testing, with the scores disaggregated by race and gender. "The soft bigotry of low expectations" was a deftly worded appeal to the breadth of the political spectrum, and NCLB passed the House 381–41 and the Senate 87–10.

NCLB espoused the express goal of improving the quality of education through standards-based accountability, and much as there is to complain about how that all worked out, it did for the first time make the achievement of marginalized students matter. Because policies intended to boost achievement of marginalized students use outcome-based data as a proxy for quality of schooling, they have inevitably exerted pressure on districts and schools to bring their educational programming in line with the tests used to produce the data. An accountability system that rewards data necessarily directs attention to the measures that produce those data. And educators who have the power to further direct attention, who are also most likely to feel the pressure from boards and the community regarding the accountability-driven data, perceive it in the best interests of the system to do so. They may be forgiven for believing that they are also acting in the best interests of students in working to improve outcomes, but this is not necessarily the case when unintended consequences are considered.

In order to increase the results on the measures that matter for accountability, some predictable changes are made that affect students' experience of school—and, we emphasize, many of the unintended consequences are invisible to the policymakers who advanced these measures as a force for positive school reform. The list of direct and indirect repercussions is fairly long; we consider the most problematic here, in the sense that they tend to have the greatest impact on already marginalized students, therefore reinforcing among equity advocates that they are right to be suspicious of data-driven efforts at improvement and make the adoption of improvement science practices less likely, although we also note that that is a small consideration compared to the impact on marginalized students.

Enacting Deficit Thinking. Accountability pressures lead to changes in curriculum, instruction, and extracurricular activities. These include the following:

- Limiting what is taught to increase time on subjects that are tested, especially reading and mathematics, to the exclusion of other subjects, such as art and other electives
- Shallowing of the curriculum within reading and mathematics to the areas that are most likely to appear on tests
- Doubling down on basic skills so that the lowest-achieving students are most likely to receive instruction that is furthest away from grade-level content

As has been pointed out by many scholars, these practices are of questionable effectiveness in terms of their intended outcomes and constrain the lived experience of marginalized students, depriving them of richness, meaning, and joy. They amount to, to use Haberman's (1991) phrase, a "pedagogy of poverty," which includes "giving information, asking questions, giving directions, making assignments, monitoring seatwork, reviewing assignments, giving tests, reviewing tests, assigning homework, reviewing homework, settling disputes, punishing noncompliance, marking papers, and giving grades." His point is not that teachers of marginalized students should not be doing these things, but that "taken together and performed to the systematic exclusion of other acts, they have become the pedagogical coin of the realm in urban schools" (p. 291).

There are other unintended consequences of sorting and ranking. For example, pull-out classes for students who receive special education services or multilingual learners may only be offered at certain times of the day, which may block students in these classes from taking honors classes offered at the same time. Assumptions are made about whether a student who qualifies for special education services under the criteria for a reading disability is able to take advanced classes in social studies or math "because of the reading required," forgetting that the whole point of Individuals with Disabilities Education Act (IDEA) and Section 504 of the Rehabilitation Act is to ensure that students are provided with accommodations and modifications so that they are able to take advantage of the full range of educational opportunities available to students who do not qualify for additional services.

Focus on Compliance. Some accountability instruments measure more than achievement. For example, many states' accountability systems include standards for attendance, and no doubt this is important, as attendance can have profound impact on grades and therefore graduation (Phillips, 2019). The trickle-down effect is that pressure is placed on administrators to ensure that procedures are followed so that the district will earn the maximum number of points allocated, which means that in some cases central office leaders make phone calls on a daily basis to schools where the taking of attendance—not the students' actual attendance, but the reporting of attendance—is less than 100%. This represents a significant dedication of resources over the course of the year to noninstructional practices. We understand why this is happening, because central office leaders are under considerable pressure to improve their accountability metrics, but also wish those resources were being devoted to improving student learning. As Labaree (1997) points out, calls for accountability have always been more focused on politics and economics than education.

Campbell's Law. The intentions of NCLB and related legislation may well have been benevolent, but they rested on strategy and assumptions that have been of dubious worth in bringing about the named outcomes. They also encouraged the corruption of data, which is a perennial threat when results count to the exclusion of all else. Of all the cases of cheating to improve test scores, the Atlanta scandal has had the most publicity, but there have been many others. Before the passage of NCLB, high-stakes accountability in Texas under Governor George Bush had already had a galvanizing effect. Among the districts that were shown not to be as impressive for all students as their overall performance suggested was Austin Independent School District (AISD). Austin High School, for example, was shown to produce achievement in Black males, on average, well below their White peers. This was surely not a new phenomenon, but it was public information for the first time. Other schools in Austin and elsewhere were eventually closed because of persistent low performance. In 1999, two senior central office leaders were indicted for manipulating test scores to make the district's performance look better.

The county attorney put his finger on the problem: "'The reality is that as we rely more on standardized testing and standardized ratings for schools there is greater and greater pressure and emphasis on obtaining the best possible rating for your school and school district,' Mr. Oden said. 'That provides greater temptation to manipulate the data in a way to create the most favorable image for your school, your district or your state''' (Whitaker, 1999).

And while we assume few have cheated, that's not all we have to worry about. Campbell's law, which County Attorney Oden paraphrased nicely, holds *that the more any quantitative social indicator is used for social decision-making, the more subject it will be to corruption pressures and the more apt it will be to distort and corrupt the social processes it is intended to monitor* (Campbell, 1979). What is ostensibly a way to pressure people to change systems is in reality a squeeze on people to change in ways they do not yet know how to do. In response, they take measures to make the data look the way they are asked to make them look, and sometimes that means making changes that are unhelpful or damaging to the people they are supposed to help, which at best is unethical and is sometimes illegal.

Relying on Lagging Indicators. If the goal is to improve learning, then the worst feature of outcomes-based accountability is that the data come too late to usefully impact instruction. The most logical approach to improvement is to get feedback as early as possible on whether a change is actually an improvement. Waiting for any kind of test takes longer than other measures that can be gathered during, or immediately following, instruction. For example, having students work on vertical nonpermanent surfaces as advocated by Liljedahl (2020) means that their thinking can be monitored by the teacher while they are working on a task; the teacher is receiving real-time feedback on student performance and can make adjustments such as making the task more or less challenging or providing additional instruction to build student capacity to do the task in the moment. And other feedback from students about their experience can be collected at the end of the lesson by a variety of methods that don't require a large amount of time to review.

Relying on Data Teams. There are many places in education where we see a weak theory of action: assumptions about the nature of the problem and solutions that also embody many assumptions about what will work. These proposed solutions are often underspecified and underestimate all the power of the solution, or fail to account for the conditions that need to be in place for the solution to have the desired effect. City et al. (2009) refer to the underspecification of the mechanism to bring about the desired result as the "and then a miracle happens" improvement theory, and this magical thinking is fully on display in the configuration of data teams.

Data teams have become almost ubiquitous in American schools. It has always been the case that teachers meet during their planning time to coplan lessons, share tactics for dealing with students who are struggling, and pool resources and knowledge. With the increased emphasis on both account-ability and equity initiated by the passage of NCLB, teacher meetings began to take on a more formal cast. The ostensible theory of action for data teams was: If teachers are provided with data about their students' achievement (usually standardized test scores), they will analyze these data, discover how they might adjust or improve their teaching practices in order to generate higher test scores by their students, and make the necessary changes in their teaching practice (Cochran-Smith & Lytle, 2009). This theory of action made several assumptions:

- *The data shed light on instruction.* Fundamental to the theory of action of data teams is that looking at data will lead in short order to improving instruction. However, many standardized tests provide information about student performance without providing sufficient actionable information about student understanding and where it may have gone off track. Knowing that a student answered many questions about fractions incorrectly does not shed light on what they don't understand, and therefore gaps in instruction are hard to diagnose.

- *Teaching is a technical challenge.* Data teams often treat the professional work of teaching as if knowing the impact of current instruction on outcome measures is easily knowable and that if teachers know about a gap between the learning objectives for their students and their students' achievement, they will know how to diagnose and fix that gap, as though classrooms function like car engines. The data may not provide answers, just clues as to what questions to ask next.

- *Teachers know how to make sense of the data.* Data teams need to know what the data they consider are telling them. However, interpreting data from standardized tests frequently requires some technical assessment literacy that teachers do not necessarily have. Furthermore, training teachers in assessment literacy may seem like a logical next step, but spending time on assessment literacy is an opportunity cost; it is an investment of time and resources that might be better spent on other topics.

- *The data reveal patterns that are applicable to future instruction rather than particular to a lesson or unit that has been taught and is not applicable to the same students.* We frequently hear school administrators say that teachers should use their data to alter their instruction, as though that data are salient for whatever lesson or unit is just about to be taught. However, this may not be the case, and spending time on "dead" data is of limited utility, especially when teachers are likely to perceive that the data "belong" to one group of students and that they cannot learn much that can be applied to future groups of students being taught the same content.

We do not believe that data teams are hopeless, merely that they have been co-opted as part of a theory of action that does not deliver on its intent, and in fact they are essential to a school focused on equity. So, in the following section, we provide some clarity on redesigning data teams more effectively as part of an improvement effort in service of equity.

RECONFIGURING DATA TEAMS TO MAKE BETTER USE OF DATA AND EMPOWER TEACHERS

Over the years since the widespread implementation of data teams, several studies have taken a closer look at how teachers make sense of achievement data and the implications for equity. Bertrand and Marsh (2015) generated a model incorporating attribution theory and sense-making theory that posits that teachers' response to data hinges on several factors, including whether they see the factors underlying the data to be under their control or not (student understanding could be under teachers' control when they see that understanding as an outcome of instruction, but not if they perceive students as slow learners or unmotivated); whether the factors are stable (for example, whether a student's identified disability is seen as a permanent feature of that student or describes only the student's current pattern of achievement); and whether the factors are internal or external to them (for example, instruction is internal, but student characteristics such as multilingual learner or qualifying for special education services are external).

Further, teachers' sense-making of data is idiosyncratic, influenced by state and district policy, leadership in their own schools, and teachers' own experience and intuition, including their biases (Datnow et al., 2012). Datnow and Park (2018) summarize the implications of the research thus: "Data-informed decision making can help schools monitor their progress toward equity goals. But we cannot simply promote data use and expect good things to happen. Educators play a critical role in shaping how and why data are used, what counts as data, and what people are aiming for when they push the use of data in schools. Data do not drive decisions by themselves" (p. 136).

Our experience with the district creation of data teams is that they tend to pay attention to structures (e.g., weekly meetings of departments or grade-level teams); logistics (e.g., the agenda for the data team meeting has to be submitted to the principal 2 days before the meeting, and the notes have to be turned in by the day after); and protocols for looking at data. Typically, less attention is given to other features that are key factors in their success and in support of equity and improvement science: empowering teachers as creators of knowledge, focusing on the system, taking a strengths-based approach, and valuing other research traditions.

Empowering Teachers as Creators of Knowledge. Our experience with data teams is that leaders expect teachers to look at data and respond without giving clear guidance as to what data they are supposed to be looking at and what they are supposed to do as a result. Such vague directions as "we want teachers to look at their data and differentiate their instruction" are not uncommon. We think that there should be a great deal more attention paid to bringing together equity and improvement science; teachers should be working together on a change idea to address a particular equity-driven problem of practice and putting that change idea to the test, having discussed in advance how they know that a change will be an improvement. We like Dylan Wiliam's (2011) framing of this: "People who espouse data-driven decision making tend to focus on the data. They collect data hoping that it might come in useful at some point in the future. Those who focus on decision-driven data collection decide what they want to do with the data before they collect it and collect only the data they need. That way, they always know what to do with the data" (p. 47).

Empowering teachers is not easy—not because teachers are not capable of working with equity-centric problems of practice, but because schools are no longer set up to support them. The tension between teachers as researchers of their own practice and as implementers of research by academics is well documented (Cochran-Smith & Lytle, 2009). Teachers are not trained as researchers and are frequently seen as not interested in research findings, for a variety of reasons (Stipek, 2005). Nevertheless, involving teachers in improving learning through various types of inquiry is not a new idea. Action research was popular in education in the 1990s and 2000s and was likely displaced, at least in part, by the new emphasis on teacher evaluation ushered in by NCLB and Race to the Top, which elevated the concept of "research-based" as knowledge about teaching that is investigated and codified by experts. So, while the role of the teacher as a creator, as well as a consumer, of knowledge has always been contested, with these new policies, practitioner inquiry was further discounted.

We find it interesting that there is so much commentary on teachers' failure to implement "with fidelity" the latest "research-based" program—with some of that commentary sympathetic and some disparaging. Yet we should also remember that if teachers had implemented every new idea that came along, they would have to forget a great deal of it. Elementary teachers with more than 10 years of experience have probably learned and unlearned at least three math programs during their tenure, and the country is in the middle of a major upheaval in the way that reading is taught. Then there are the other "research-based" ideas that have not been shown to be effective at scale, including differentiation and learning styles, which still linger in teacher practice.

While action research, practitioner inquiry, and various forms of continuous improvement involving teachers have never gone away entirely, they have been supplanted by much more outcomes-focused visions of what teacher communities of practice should look like. And while these visions are frequently driven by the desire for achievement to improve, especially among marginalized students, they often ignore the reality and the complexity of connecting teaching practices to student learning. So, data teams, professional learning communities, or communities of practice must balance academic research and theory, knowledge of the system, and knowledge of practitioners (Bryk et al., 2015). The work of data teams cannot be disconnected from research, nor can it be separate from organization-level goals, but it also cannot view teachers as implementers of research without powerful tacit knowledge of their own to contribute.

Focusing on the System. We have already pointed out that educational leaders have almost certainly been exposed to ideas about systems thinking. And yet, on a daily basis, almost all of them participate in a performance-based system that sees low-achieving students as the problem and seeks to "fix" them through leveraging grading policy and practices; attendance policy, incentives, and punishments; and course assignments and instruction that establish standardized measures of achievement as the gatekeepers to rich learning experiences. Improvement science offers a process that looks at any and all outcomes as created by a system and states that blaming the individuals in the system for those outcomes is illogical, inefficient, ineffective, and morally wrong (Deming, 1982). While we suspect that most data team advocates would see data teams as being about the system, our experience is that they are much more about single-loop than double-loop learning (Argyris, 1977). When data teams are given permission to be equity-focused and to ask questions that challenge the workings of the system, then responsibility shifts from the students to figure out how to work within the system to making the system work for them.

We could give examples here of how data teams have realized, for instance, that students from a certain part of town are more likely to be tardy or absent in bad weather because the sidewalks are hazardous. But frequently, that sort of knowledge is already known in the school, but there is no mechanism for collating that information and sharing it with leaders at the district level who are in a position to advocate for fixing potholes or erecting traffic barriers or hiring crossing guards. Data teams are frequently construed as being the work of teachers, but systems are nested, and teacher-level data teams should also be connected to other lines of communication that run across the system.

For example, a school may have a goal of improving on-track performance of 9th-graders (i.e., having the credits, including in gatekeeper subjects like Algebra 1 or English 1 to be promoted to 10th grade in 1 year). One way to go about this is to focus on student capacity to navigate the system as it currently exists—getting them to come to school, getting them to get to class on time, convincing them of the importance of turning in homework, etc. Another way to go about this is to question the assumptions and values on which these systems are based—for example, questioning the logic, biases, and values of grading practices, scheduling, or instruction, if the data indicate that the systems are generating inequity.

Data teams are often asked to jump to plans without examining the system as a whole or questioning why it operates the way it does. It is easy to generate a to-do list that does not address problems and solutions at a system or program level and focus instead on the immediate and the logistical. Issues around equity appear to spark the need to demonstrate "a sense of urgency" that is actually counterproductive when it means that data teams always feel like they are under the gun to create and execute plans. Data teams and school improvement teams are frequently required to write plans on an annual basis that are disconnected from the work of the previous year—sometimes they are explicitly told that what they are already doing does not need to be in the plan, that they should list only new work, as though what they did last year does not matter.

Again, we are not suggesting that outcomes are not important, nor that standardized test scores are not important. Indeed, the excellent teachers studied by Gloria Ladson-Billings (1995) in her study of culturally relevant pedagogy were identified as excellent in part because of the standardized test scores achieved by their students. Nevertheless, the theory of action that we endorse is very different from the hard-edged accountability of "if we establish ambitious goals and hold people accountable (i.e., reward and punish), then those goals will be met." Data teams that are designed to focus on outcomes at the expense of understanding the relationship between teaching and learning tend to focus on quick fixes and do not challenge the systems that produce those outcomes. If an organization can articulate a strategy that it has faith in over the long term, then it will encourage educators to establish goals around learning to implement that strategy and garner feedback from them about the effectiveness of the strategy (Stevenson & Weiner, 2021).

We have written extensively already about the reasons for paying attention to student experience in the collection and analysis of data: students' sense of belonging; their insights into instruction; their treatment—fairly or unfairly, respectful or disrespectful, supportive or unhelpful—by teachers, counselors, and administrators; and their input into school goals, policies, and practices. We have argued that we should be centering student experience because it gives us insight into how the system operates—the expectations that adults in the system have for students—and because it is the right thing to do. Now we want to add one more reason: Data from students provide us with leading indicators of the impact of change. Listening to the experience of students gives us early data about shifts in the system, whether these shifts are instructional, disciplinary, or cultural.

Embracing an Asset-Based View of Students. Obviously, we believe that all educational goals should have an equity component; if educators are not working toward a goal of improvement for all students but particularly for marginalized students, then our institutions will continue to reproduce inequity. However, beyond the goals, there are concepts and practices that we think are useful for teachers to know and use. Many school and district leaders are very aware of the use of deficit-driven language among teachers—we know this because we hear them complain about it so often. But few have practices that enable more equity-focused discussions without blaming teachers. For example, some schools have a deliberate practice of changing the pronoun "they" to "we" when discussing professional practice; this has the effect of framing problems and solutions in terms of adult action. Rather than locating problems and/or solutions in the students ("they need to be more motivated"), or even the teachers ("teachers need to have a growth mindset"), the educators in a data team take ownership of those problems and solutions ("we need to make sure our grading policies are more consistent; we need to make sure that teachers have a shared understanding of what high-quality instruction looks like; we need to create the conditions for all students to feel like they belong"). It is a fundamental shift to think of students as strategic and prudent thinkers who are making logical choices in response to their environments.

Measuring What Really Matters. The outcomes that are the basis of outcomes-based accountability do matter, because those outcomes are also gatekeepers to further opportunities for students, including, of course, college entrance. But if an outcomes-based accountability system leads to an impoverished experience of schooling for marginalized students, then the focus has to shift. Here, we have found Stiggins and DuFour's (2009) idea of matching the type of assessment to the needs of the stakeholders to be a useful heuristic for deciding which stakeholders should be paying attention to which data. At the institutional level, boards of education and superintendents need outcomes-based assessment data in order to make budget and policy decisions about direction of resources and plans. At the program level, principals, department chairs, and teacher teams need information to tell them whether their plans for improvement are being enacted as planned and whether these plans are leading to improvement for students. And at the classroom level, teachers and students need continuous information about individual students' academic progress and experience of schooling.

The implication for data teams is that educators should be considering data that they have control over. Asking teachers to "reflect" on standardized test scores can only give them the most general information about where students are as opposed to where we would like them to be. And data teams need not be constrained by outcome data. Educators are so accustomed to outcome-based measures, usually standardized tests, that they appear unaware that there are other ways of knowing, yet there are many well-respected works that discuss alternative epistemologies—see, for example, Gilligan (1982) and Collins (2022), whose four-part framework is particularly helpful: lived experience as a criterion of meaning, the use of dialogue in assessing knowledge claims, the ethics of caring, and the ethic of personal responsibility. They also have a mental model of research that specifies that randomized control studies are the "gold standard" (Hariton & Locascio, 2018). And yet, there are many other possibilities, discussed in the following section.

A WORD ON EQUITY AUDITS

In their highly influential article, Skrla et al. (2004) described a process for conducting an equity audit predicated on the idea that achievement equity is the sum of teacher equity (i.e., the assignment of effective teachers across and within schools such that the lowest-achieving students are not further disadvantaged by being assigned the least effective teachers) plus programmatic equity (i.e., ensuring that students of color and students from low-income homes are not overrepresented regarding special education services, are making adequate progress when they participate in bilingual education, are not discriminated against regarding the application and consequences of student discipline, and are not underrepresented regarding gifted and talented programs). They provide a full justification for their approach, but nevertheless many of the data they propose using for the purposes of measuring teacher quality are decidedly flawed proxies. Perhaps for that reason, but perhaps also because of the politics of even raising the issue of variation in teacher quality, let alone measuring it, equity audits have become a standard part of the repertoire of "working on equity" while the method advocated by Skrla et al. has not.

In our experience, most equity audits are confined to the organization of data that already exist within a school or district, such as standardized test scores, incidence of in-school or out-of-school suspensions, attendance, and graduation rates. These data are then forwarded to a district equity team, or school data teams, with the assumption and expectation that something will be done, although occasionally, a district goes to the trouble of undertaking a much more comprehensive equity audit, perhaps hiring an external consultant to collect and analyze data from student focus groups, administer staff and community surveys, and organize data into infographics, to name a few typical activities. Often, these are intended to lay the groundwork for a new strategic plan, or to create a sense of urgency around a district focus on equity, or to provide a new superintendent with a rationale for making changes to district policy or programming. We completely understand and relate to these reasons. At the same time, the big, performative nature of such audits makes them events rather than processes, and it is easy to let the data collected and reported to be underutilized in the absence of routines that are put in place to address the inequity that has been identified.

So, while we recognize that there may be a good reason to embark on the "event" version of an equity audit, we want to emphasize that it may be the precursor to, but it cannot replace, the routine of continuous improvement.

AT YOUR DESK OR IN THE HALLS

The history of data use is complicated and fraught. And on top of that, the institutional logic of education reform cleaves tightly to the belief that outcome-based, standardized data are superior to all other forms. But we believe there are rich opportunities for gathering data that reflect the breadth and depth of student experience without abandoning data collection altogether. Educators have also been taught that to be data-driven is a good thing, somehow forgetting that a moral use of data must provide information leading to the enhancement of the educational experience of marginalized students, not to their further marginalization.

Reflection Questions

- What is my current relationship with data? How have traditional views of data shaped my practice?
- This chapter discussed how data have historically been used for discriminatory purposes. What are the practical implications for data use in my school or district?
- How do I suspend certainty when analyzing and making sense of data?
- Which types of data do I prioritize over others? Why do I believe those are more important than others?
- What systems and routines currently exist to support my collection and analysis of qualitative data—particularly stories from the margins?

CHAPTER 8

The Absolute Necessity
of Conversation

"But no matter how daunting, you are here because you want to hear and
you want to be heard. You are here because you know that something is very
wrong and you want a change. We can find our way to each other. We can
find a way to our truths. I have seen it happen. My life is a testament to it.
And it all starts with conversation."

—Oluo, 2018, p. 6

Change is fractal. Leaders and researchers and consultants talk about
organizational change, and indeed many aspects of change happen at
an organizational level, including policies and processes and routines
and the vision and mission of the organization. But ultimately change is
brought about by individuals; in order for improvement to take place,
real people producing outcomes that matter have to do things differently. And in almost all cases, people don't change just because there's a
change in policy. People change because of conversations. Organizational
change is the product of individual change multiplied across many individuals, which means that many conversations have to happen. In this
chapter, then, we talk about what it takes to have productive conversations that lead to meaningful improvement in the schooling of marginalized students.

Unfortunately, education reform tends to focus on more abstract, psychologically distant plans and policies, and not enough attention is paid to
changing practice and having the necessary conversations to do that collectively and collaboratively. Improvement that centers equity requires knowing what it will take to understand the experience of students, educators,
parents, and community members who have been marginalized and to use
that understanding to make some quite profound changes. Understanding
experience is impossible to imagine without conversation. Surveys, data collection, equity audits—all of these carry so much more meaning when accompanied by people's stories. And to know people's stories, you have to
listen to them.

We work with people to lower their expectations about having conversations they are not confident about having; we are trying, in other words, to lower the stakes. Educators tend to be very focused on the expectation that these conversations "go well." But holding to that standard means that many conversations are avoided completely because people are worried that they won't go well. Perhaps the criterion for success is not that the conversation "goes well," but that it happens at all. Rather than waiting until a future date when you have acquired the skills you think you need, it is much more important to engage these conversations with good intent and to start small, perhaps with empathy interviews or within the structure of a closely held protocol. As with any skill, you need practice, and it is impossible to acquire the skill through knowledge alone.

In this chapter, we explore what can make conversations about equity difficult and how you can build the capacity to have productive conversations about race and other emotionally triggering topics. If you haven't already guessed, we think that the ability to have conversations is underappreciated and that the prevalence of the ability to have conversations is overestimated. The skills involved in listening to one another, even without the added freight of high-stakes topics, are not innate, and yet we frequently hear admonitions to "just talk to the person" or "give them feedback," as if these things are easy, simple, and come naturally. So, let's elucidate some of the complications.

WHY CONVERSATIONS ABOUT RACE ARE SO DIFFICULT

There is no doubt that conversations about race are often fraught. There are plenty of conversations that are difficult that aren't about race, but race brings its own particular set of challenges. Here we talk about what these are, but we preface this by saying that the chances of having productive conversations about race (which may still be difficult) increase when you have some practice having hard conversations, and also conversations that require more metacognition than simply the casual conversation you might have at church, or even the planning or other work conversations you have daily.

A metacognitive conversation is one in which you have to pay attention to your thoughts and feelings as well as the topic at hand. Here are some examples, only slightly adapted from our own experiences.

Your aunt Mabel's daughter is about to finish her medical residency and become an oncologist at a teaching hospital. Aunt Mabel is justifiably proud but also can't help making small and frequent comments about your own career that imply that you ought to be proud of your cousin, envious of her achievements, and regretful of your own life choices. You love Aunt

Mabel, and she has a right to be proud of her daughter, and so you pay attention to any feelings of resentment that crop up when she makes these jabs at you and maintain a smiling face and an admiring tone.

Your boss gives pretty good advice, and his feedback is generally helpful, but sometimes the way he goes about giving feedback about something he wants you to do differently is just annoying. He leads with, "So, how do you think that went?," which is code for, "I have things to say but I'm going to follow the mental model I have for feedback, which is that I should ask you for your thoughts first, which I'm really not going to listen to, but I will have done what I think I'm supposed to do." Plus, the things he thinks you did wrong are often the same things you've seen him do, and you think it's amazing that he seems oblivious to that. So, as much as you are tempted to give what we call "boomerang feedback," which is feedback that you send right back at the other person, you dutifully write down everything he says and thank him for his input.

Your friend's husband died after a long illness, and you spend a lot of time with her as she grieves, sometimes helping with the kids, sometimes holding her hand while she cries, but mostly listening to her talk, which you are glad to do. However, your mother died just a week before your friend's husband, yet she seems completely unaware that you too are grieving and that it might be hard for you to absorb all the emotion she is sharing with you or that you might like it if she asked how you were doing occasionally. But you know that, at this moment, she does not really have the same capacity that you do, so you continue to show up for your friend and deal with your own grief through other avenues.

And these examples aren't explicitly about race. But they could be about race. If your aunt Mabel is White and you are Black, her comments can have racial overtones—that she is implying that stereotypes that have always been in play for Black people—not as smart, not as dedicated, a little lazy—are true for you, too. If your boss is a Black woman, it may be particularly hard for her to give feedback to a White man, as it is quite likely that her competence has been questioned in the past, even by her direct reports, who tend to be far more willing to question a Black woman in authority than a Black man or a White woman. And so, it is less surprising that her approach to feedback might come across as stiff, procedural, and overly officious.

THE PRIVILEGE OF COMFORT

We frequently hear—usually, but not always—from White people that they don't want to feel uncomfortable or don't want others to feel uncomfortable. "Comfort" is an umbrella term that is used to explain and excuse avoidance of any conversation that may cause discomfort. Physical comfort is easy to describe; it is mostly about what is absent: pain, hunger, thirst, exhaustion, constraint, extreme cold or heat, and so on. Emotional comfort is likewise about what is absent: stress, loneliness, grief, embarrassment, shame, despair, anxiety, and so on. Comfort, then, is a low bar. So, when people say they are uncomfortable having certain conversations, what do they mean? They mean that they are experiencing stress or anxiety, which shows up physiologically as an elevated heart rate, sweaty palms, tense muscles, difficulty swallowing, dry mouth, lightheadedness, or nausea. Usually, these feelings and symptoms are mild; nevertheless, they are unpleasant enough that people are motivated to avoid them. The underlying causes of discomfort can be one or more of the following:

- White people are under stereotype threat (Steele, 2010). The stereotype they are battling is that White people are clueless when it comes to race, don't understand their privilege, and stumble through the world blissfully ignorant of the racism, at multiple levels, that people of color experience, and add to that experience by speaking and acting according to their mental models of people of color. Not wanting to fulfill that stereotype is cognitively demanding, because it means that you are having a particularly fraught metacognitive conversation; in other words, the social costs of saying or doing the wrong thing are high. Saying the wrong thing when it comes to talking about race may mean being seen as clueless at best and racist at worst. And for most White people, there is particular dread attached to being considered racist, as being racist is uniquely shameful (Pollock, 2004).
- For White people and people of color, this is not a conversation they feel safe to have. Discussions about race, dis/ability, and sexuality are frequently emotionally charged and nuanced. People from marginalized groups may fear retaliation if they "make life difficult" for someone in power by raising a concern or making a complaint—doubly so if the person in power is the cause for concern. People with privilege relative to the issue are often worried about saying something offensive, revealing ignorance, or being unaware of their privilege. Concern about being misinterpreted, misrepresented, or misunderstood is a powerful constraint on feeling comfortable to speak. Previous experience matters: Have I been ignored, dismissed, derided, embarrassed, shamed, or humiliated? Or have I felt seen, heard, supported, validated, appreciated, applauded, and given grace? And then there is how I perceive others in the conversation: what I believe to be their intent, motivation, hubris/humility, flexibility, mood, and ability to listen and whether I feel safe with them or whether I fear judgment.

- This is not a conversation White people think they should be having. Not so long ago, there were topics that were undiscussable beyond the bounds of immediate family: suicide, some types of cancer, AIDS, depression, homosexuality, menstruation, abortion. Taboo is perhaps too strong a word, but it was simply not socially acceptable to have these conversations in "polite company." And despite the fact that many of these facets of human experience now appear on sitcoms and reality TV shows, many of these topics are still limited to immediate family (especially regarding mental and physical illnesses that carry some connotation of weakness or shame) or same-gender friendship groups (especially regarding sexuality and reproduction). For people brought up to think that color-blind is the right stance to take, conversations about race may feel inappropriate and therefore embarrassing.
- This is not a conversation they have the experience to have. For White people especially, race is a trait that people of color carry, not something that applies to them. White people believe that because they have never been racially profiled or discriminated against, that racism is not part of their experience. They may not have considered that racism is something that they benefit from and may resent the concept of privilege because they did not "come from privilege," see their own success as only about their own hard work, and cannot see the tailwinds that push them forward (Davidai & Gilovich, 2016). They believe, therefore, that there is nothing they can contribute to a conversation about race, and therefore should not be expected to participate.
- People who have had conversations about equity that have "gone well" are more willing and likely to have similar conversations in the future. Continued perceived success leads to the willingness to have even more conversations, which affords the development of more skill, which leads to more success, and so forth. Perceived self-efficacy, successful outcomes, and further opportunities are part of a virtuous cycle. This is not a conversation they have the vocabulary for. They have had no education, experience, or training that has equipped them with the necessary language and concepts to talk about race.

White people are, therefore, particularly motivated to avoid conversations about race. People from privileged backgrounds and in higher-status positions are better able to avoid conversations that make them feel uncomfortable, because they assert their power in order to decide what is discussed and what is not. For people of color, conversations about race tend to be difficult, and exhausting, because they are the ones who frequently bear the cognitive and emotional burden of the metacognitive conversation, not least because they are seen to be the cause of discomfort. A White person who does not wish to feel uncomfortable and who also sees race as something that does not inhere in them attaches discomfort in having conversations about race to people of color.

To be clear, we do not mean to disparage White people who avoid conversations about race. For them, the social stakes are high, and they are often ill-prepared to enter conversations about equity that entail talking about race—and ironically, the legislatures in many states are working hard to make it even less likely that they will be prepared. But we do think that they bear the burden of equipping themselves to have conversations about race—and indeed, other "uncomfortable" topics.

CONVERSATION SKILLS

Neither of us has ever run a marathon, but we think that it's a good metaphor for what we're talking about here. We can't imagine that anyone would wake up one day and say, "I think I'll run a marathon this weekend." A marathon is a pretty significant challenge, and runners prepare for them over the course of several months. You have to build up the aerobic capacity to run that far for that long, and your muscles and tendons need to be very strong, so you just have to put in the miles, week after week, perhaps running several times during the week and for an increasingly long amount of time on weekends.

We see conversations about race and equity as analogous to running a marathon. We don't think it's advisable to make a conversation about equity your first metacognitive conversation, in the same way that your first run should not be 26.2 miles. Many of the lessons that are outputs from all one's life experiences so far are inputs to having meaningful conversations. Here are some examples from our own lives.

We have sat with people who are grieving, and we have talked to them about what they need and don't need. We have learned that there is nothing that we can say that is guaranteed to make the other person feel better and several hundred things that can make them feel worse, so we keep quiet. We don't put the other person in the position of having to manage our emotions as well as their own, such as when the person who is grieving feels the need to assure us that they are doing okay, because they infer that that would make us feel better. We know that physical touch may be what they need, but it may not, so we make it easy for them to take our hand or lean on our shoulder without invading their space. And we know that some people communicate that they are discomfited by strong emotion, which makes the person who is grieving feel like there is something embarrassing or shameful about that emotion, so we do not look away from grief.

We have listened to angry parents who are upset about their child's experience with a staff member or another child. We have learned that they are insulted if they feel like we are minimizing their concerns, even when we don't think that that's what we are doing; we may think that we are explaining something that they don't understand or providing some context, but they may interpret this response as defensiveness, or denial, or us simply not listening to them. We have learned that it may be equally insulting to try to manage their emotions, thereby giving them the impression that we think they are overreacting, or overwrought, or irrational.

Having conversations about equity inevitably entails difficult conversations, in the sense that they are going to elicit emotions that you'd rather avoid. Hearing about someone else's trauma can be upsetting because you may feel sad, powerless, or guilty. Listening to someone be angry at something that has been done to them, whether or not you did it, can make you feel defensive. Dealing with extreme emotions, such as anger, despair, or disgust, can lead you to want to deflect those emotions, which can lead you to dismiss them as unreasonable or irrational, which can lead you to be dismissive of the person communicating those emotions.

Nothing prepares you for having meaningful conversations like experience with meaningful conversations. There is supposedly a Chinese proverb that says the best time to plant a tree was 20 years ago and the second-best time is today. We feel the same way about conversations. Training in the skills described next is important, but challenging conversations cannot, and should not, wait until the training has happened. Lack of training is not an excuse for failure to advocate on behalf of marginalized students.

We are aware that some of what we tell you here is contrary to what you may have been told elsewhere. Before we consider those details, we want to remind you of the point of Chapter 6: There is a very long and ugly history in the United States of ignoring, infantilizing, and ridiculing people from marginalized groups who had the audacity to point out that they had a case for a different interpretation of facts, a more righteous course of action, and the right to be heard. And just because this is the history does not mean it is all in the past: Numerous studies still show that women; people of color; people with disabilities; and people who fall outside societal norms for sexuality, family groups, and gender identity still experience microaggressions of all kinds. One of the most common is that they are not listened to, but are ignored, or talked over, or "mansplained," and its equivalents.

Listening. There is no end of advice easily available about how to be a good listener. And yet, we believe that much of it is not about what really matters. So rather than getting caught up in behaviors that are designed to indicate that you are listening, such as paraphrasing what someone just said, paying attention to body language, and trying to show interest through your facial expression, we think you should just listen closely to people and work hard to understand what they are saying. The one behavior we encourage is to ask salient questions, because they will help you be a better listener and because people report feeling listened to more when the listener asks polite, relevant questions.

Listening, then, may seem like a low bar for basic good manners, but, amazingly enough, it is a level of respect that many people cannot take for granted. We point all this out as a reminder that how people in power handle listening to people with less power than they have holds a much greater significance than they sometimes realize and that leaders would do well to act accordingly. It's also worth noting that the issue of respect does not apply only when listening to students and community members or to members of marginalized groups. A survey of nearly 20,000 employees in companies around the world found that respect is the leadership behavior that has the largest effect on employee engagement and commitment—more important even than recognition and appreciation; communicating an inspiring vision; or opportunities for learning, growth, and development (Porath, 2015).

Listening happens at several different levels. There is the kind of listening that happens at the barber shop, when the conversation starts with talking about sports, which reminds someone of what happens at their grandmother's 65th birthday party, which somehow ends up as a conversation about who is going to win the next presidential election. The kind of listening that we are concerned with is much more purposeful; there is a tacit but shared understanding that the conversation is going somewhere, that the speaker has specific information they want to convey, and that the function of the listener is to support the thinking of the other person.

Listening has acquired many adjectives: active listening, empathetic listening, deep listening, strategic listening, and so on. From our perspective, listening is both a means and an end. We listen because we want to understand the other person, but also because listening is an act of compassion and respect. Listening has several purposes, including but not limited to listening to learn, listening to understand, listening to care, and listening to problem-solve.

As part of the Introduction to Coaching Institute that we hold, we give participants homework: to listen to someone that they have a hard time listening to. They don't have to fix a problem or fix the relationship or coach the person—they just have to listen. Then we ask them to debrief the experience during the next session. This is always one of the most moving parts of the institute, and sometimes it is life-changing.

The pitfalls with listening are many. Some people find it hard not to use what they hear as a springboard to start talking about what they think is important or give their point of view. Others find it difficult not to give advice. Still others ask questions that have more to do with leading the speaker to a particular way of thinking or seeing. Some think of listening as what they need to do in order to have someone else listen to them; of course, listening should not be transactional, but we still see advice in leadership and coaching resources that you should listen to someone *so that* they will be more open to hearing your perspective. And some people find silence extremely hard to tolerate and will jump into spaces in a conversation just to fill the gaps. Listening is, therefore, actually quite challenging to do well and requires practice.

A search of *Harvard Business Review* returns 120 articles with the word "listen" in the title. And, not surprisingly for a magazine with leaders for an audience, many of those articles are about making it safe for others to tell leaders the bad news (see, for example, Bryant & Sharer, 2021). Listening is, therefore, very much connected to other essential concepts, but especially that of psychological safety: People who believe that there will be consequences for telling the truth as they see it, or even just for telling you something they think you don't want to hear, will choose to keep quiet. A useful heuristic for leaders, when asking questions to better understand processes or experiences, is to avoid "who/why" questions (implying blame) and to ask "how/what" questions (focused on the process) instead (Toussaint & Barnas, 2021).

Pay Attention. Probably the most obvious thing we can tell you is that you should give the other person in the conversation your full attention, which means putting away your phone and preventing other distractions, because you have limited cognitive capacity, and anything that increases the load on that capacity means that you have less to devote elsewhere. As Kahneman (2011) puts it: "The often-used phrase 'pay attention' is apt: you dispose of a limited budget of attention that you can allocate to activities, and if you try to go beyond your budget, you will fail" (p. 23). It also means letting go of the myth that you can multitask (Tokuhama-Espinosa, 2018); you can chat with your friend on the phone while doing the dishes, but you cannot pay close attention to what is being said and do something else at the same time. Sound is also a distraction. In many workshop settings, background music is played during small-group discussions or breakout sessions, and that can make it harder to listen.

Beyond cognitive capacity, paying attention means listening to what the other person is saying right now, which means staying in the present with them. And in order to do that, you have to not think about other things, which is where our advice differs from a lot of other advice you will get about listening. Frequently, the advice is that you should nod as the other person is speaking, interject affirmations such as "mm-hm" and "right," and paraphrase what the person has told you, typically by beginning, "What I hear you say is . . ." However, these behaviors may come across as formulaic and patronizing and may irritate or inflame someone who is already upset. But just as importantly, the cognitive effort that you put into listening in order to paraphrase or otherwise demonstrate that you are listening is diverting effort that you should be putting into actually listening.

The other behavior that consumes cognitive resources is formulating what you are going to say in response to the other person while they are still talking to you. Planning for the future takes you out of the present and severely hinders your ability to fully take in what someone else is trying to tell you. This, however, is a very hard habit to break. Leaders are rewarded for having the right answer, which makes it harder for them to be in the moment because they have to live up to the expectations people have of them. Leaders who have been conditioned to always be in control and to have the right answer and know the right thing to say at all times do not like the idea of letting go of those norms in order to "be in the moment," which sounds New Age-y and formless. And yet, you cannot know what someone is going to say until they have actually said it, and to have an immediate comeback is to concede that you have anticipated, rather than considered, the meaning of their speech. Better, we argue, to be authentic than polished, especially when what is authentic is also respectful.

Manage Your Emotions. As we discussed in Chapter 5, we become defensive when we believe that we are somehow at risk. This could be a suggestion that we have done something wrong or embarrassing or the inference that our intentions are tainted. It's also very stressful to feel that you have been, or are being, misunderstood. When we believe that we are in the presence of some kind of threat to our sense of ourselves as well-meaning, competent, caring professionals, the temptation to react defensively is almost overwhelming. There is a plethora of defensive routines that we can employ to extricate ourselves from the threat. Yoshino and Glasgow (2023) organize these into what they call "the four conversational traps":

- *Avoid.* When the conversation is just too stressful or embarrassing, or when people don't have answers to questions, they may simply refuse to engage. We were recently asked to join a senior leadership team that had been having conversations about equity, race, and antiracism. We were going to help set the stage for linking their equity work with the planning sessions that were on the calendar for them to create their strategic plan. However, the planning group with whom we'd been working apparently did not tell the executive director that this conversation was going to take place, because when we started asking questions about the connections between their work on equity and the strategic plan, the executive director became quite agitated, and a few minutes later declared, "The equity work and the strategic plan are two separate things and we're going to deal with them separately. Got it? Thanks."
- *Deflect.* There are multiple ways to deflect. For example, DiAngelo (2018) has documented the behavior of White people

who become upset when racism is discussed; they may cry out of sympathy for what others have endured, or complain that they are being made to feel like they are the problem when they have no control over the history of racism, or equate hardship they have experienced in their lives with exposure to bigotry or racial discrimination experienced by people of color. We are not suggesting that these feelings are not real, nor that they are only about deflection—simply that they also have the effect of deflecting the conversation away from racism (or any other "painful" topic). Another deflection tactic is to criticize the tone in which a statement is made, rather than the truth of the statement—this is known as tone policing. In a kind of discriminatory double-play, tone policing can also play into racist stereotypes, as when a Black woman's concerns are dismissed because her tone is angry, or a Black man is told his arguments are weak or don't make sense, or a woman who is complaining of sexual harassment is told she is being hysterical. Deflection is also in operation when someone responds to a statement by asking, "Yes, but what about. . . ." The effect is to turn the conversation away from the concern being raised to another topic, which may be an authentic issue, but is being used as an escape from the topic that is thereby ignored. This defensive reaction is known, elegantly, as "whataboutism."

- *Deny.* Another common tactic is to simply deny there is a problem. We once worked with a high school math department; the curriculum department at the district level was disturbed by the number of math courses in total, many of which were not rigorous, and the sequences into which the courses were organized, which meant that to be able to enroll in upper-level courses, students had to take Honors Algebra in 8th grade. We devised an activity in which the teachers created a flow chart of the math courses. Our theory was that once they saw the implications of how the courses were ranked and organized, they would feel a little sheepish and would realize that they needed to restructure the program of studies in math. This, however, is not what happened. Instead of realizing that inequity was built into the system, they talked about how proud they were of the number of courses they were offering, even though that meant multiple preps, and couldn't see what the problem was.

- *Attack.* Sometimes, defensive reactions are ugly. They are ad hominem attacks: disparaging comments about the person, not about what they are saying. These can range from the mild "Who does she think she is?" to more aggressive accusations of being stupid, being ignorant, or acting in bad faith. They are usually reactions by someone who is insulted, offended, embarrassed, ashamed, or completely at a loss. The more public the emotion, the more likely attacking will be the reaction.

All of these reactions have a similar effect, in that they direct attention away from the contentious topic, which, if nothing else, is convenient for the person who feels at risk in the conversation. And as DiAngelo (2018) points out, the attention shifts to those who consider themselves injured by the conversation, perceiving that they have been made to feel bad and are entitled to feel comfortable and be comforted.

Be Humble. The movie *Moneyball* includes many scenes in which baseball scouts make predictions about how good a player is going to be based on questionable indicators, such as the attractiveness of their girlfriends. And they are pretty confident in their predictions. And as documented in the book of the same name (Lewis, 2004), those conversations may have been fictionalized, but they are not far from what used to happen, and probably still does. At one point in the movie, the general manager, Billy Beane, who had personal experience with the overconfidence of scouts, says to one of the scouts: "You think you know, but you don't. You don't." Our lack of awareness of the gaps in our knowledge and perception is a major barrier to learning through conversation. We need to consciously cultivate the humility to recognize that our sense of what is true in any given situation may be thoroughly distorted (Toussaint & Barnas, 2021).

Don't Tell People How They Feel. As we discussed in Chapter 2, many texts on listening and coaching advise the listener to pay attention to body language and facial expressions. You can still find in many books about coaching and leadership the statistic that 7% of the meaning of a message is communicated by words, 38% by tone of voice, and 55% by body language. This comes from the work of Albert Mehrabian (1981), but his findings have been so overgeneralized as to become meaningless. In fact, Mehrabian was reporting on very limited circumstances, in which the tone of the voice of the speaker is inconsistent with the meaning of one word, and only one word. Thus, the context in which the experiments were conducted is almost never applicable in real life.

Barrett (2017) has shown that the relationship between facial expression, body language, and emotion is not as clear-cut as commonly assumed. We think that we can determine how people feel by the look on their face, their posture, or their folded arms, but we have a false sense of certainty about how correct we are.

Eyal et al. (2018) report that the commonly used tactic of "perspective taking" is not a reliable way to increase your understanding of what someone else is thinking or feeling. They report 25 experiments that test whether being instructed to look at a situation from someone else's point of view increases insight. In fact, perspective taking appeared to have the opposite effect—it had a tendency to decrease the accuracy of prediction of how someone else was feeling or what they were thinking; at the same time, being asked to take someone else's perspective increased people's confidence that they knew what the other person was thinking or feeling. What appears to happen when we look at things from someone else's perspective is that our interpretation is less egocentric, but we replace that egocentrism with an inference about the other person that may or may not be correct. Perspective taking is no guarantee of accuracy; you are still guessing what the other person is thinking.

Similarly, you can find guidance about how people from different cultures behave, presumably so that you have a better understanding of what they are thinking and feeling. There are two problems here. First, while it is certainly true that norms vary across cultures, those norms are generalizations that may not hold true for individuals within that culture. For example, visitors to the United States may be told that Americans greet each other with a firm handshake, but that behavior varies across and within social groups, has subtle differences between genders, and may not be a practice of some individuals at all. If an American does not shake hands with you, it is probably not a deliberate show of disrespect. Second, the promulgation of generalizations about behavioral norms risks perpetuating stereotypes that are not necessarily helpful in promoting cross-cultural understanding and may have the opposite effect. The only way to know how someone feels is to ask them. And yet, in our coaching work, we find that participants are very happy to make inferences about what is going on in someone's head from very vague clues. At every coaching workshop there is demonstration coaching, and the debrief inevitably involves observers making statements such as, "I could tell that you were unhappy she said that when you crossed your arms"; "That must have been hard to hear"; "You were really squirming during those long silences." As we pointed out in Chapter 7, how we know is who we are, and the assumptions we make about the meaning of others' gestures, posture, and body language are simply a reflection of our mental models.

CONVERSATION: WHERE THE BIG IDEAS COME TOGETHER

Most people spend significant chunks of their waking hours in conversation with others. It may seem silly, therefore, to explain how to have a conversation. And yet we know from working with so many dedicated educators over the years that people are aware that some types of conversation are harder than others, that some topics of conversation are harder than others, and therefore they do not always feel that they have the capacity to have those hard conversations. We see the concepts discussed in previous chapters as the foundation for conversations about equity, and that conversational skill cannot be separated from knowledge and dispositions; learning conversational skill is necessary but not sufficient to feel confident in your capacity to talk to anybody about anything. So, let's take a look at the bricks in the foundation, where they appear elsewhere in the book, and why they are important.

We talked about mental models in Chapter 1, and here we bring them up again, because our mental models are intricately woven into how we think and also into how we feel, which has direct bearing on our ability to converse about a range of topics. You may have read in books and articles talking about "difficult" or "sensitive" topics about "fight, flight, or freeze" reactions to a perceived threat or about an "amygdala hijack," as though these reactions were beyond our control. But these reactions are moderated by what we think and how we think.

It may be the case that we have an instinctual reaction to seeing a tiger that causes a physiological response that readies us to make a run for it. But there are not many tigers in our everyday lives. Normally, we have to think about a situation in a certain way in order to feel about it in a certain way. For example, to be embarrassed about something I've done, I need to realize that I've done something wrong or socially unacceptable; that I've been "caught" (i.e., what I've done has come to the attention of others); that they will judge me; that the judgment will reflect poorly on me in some way; and that there is some kind of social cost that I will pay. Similarly, in order to be insulted, I need to recognize that someone has said or done something disrespectful, scornful, or abusive; that there was intent attached to the speech or action; and that I care enough about the speaker/actor and/or the words or actions to be upset by them, perhaps because the person holds a lot of power or the insult is highly derogatory. In other words, the link between event and emotion is not simple or linear, and it involves a lot of cognition.

It is possible, therefore, to change the way you feel about a situation by changing the way you think. And, therefore, to a certain extent you choose how you feel. This is, of course, quite difficult to do; our thoughts, beliefs, and mental models cannot be switched on and off like a light. But you can ask yourself, "What is the story I told myself about this situation?" to at least raise awareness that there are multiple possible interpretations and the one you are choosing to apply is just that: a choice among many.

In Chapter 2 we wrote at length about empathy, and in Chapter 3 we described other personal dispositions. These are crucial for talking with someone else about a topic that might challenge your worldview or the way you see yourself. We have also written about the existing mental model that dispositions are traits that we are born with rather than skills that we might acquire. Having conversations about "uncomfortable" topics can very quickly become wrapped up with how we see ourselves: "I'm no good at talking to strangers"; "I'm not the kind of person who can handle emotional subjects"; "I'm too much of an introvert for that kind of thing." Mindsets are beliefs about our own psychology, and we can shift our mindsets. Most educators are familiar with the work of Carol Dweck (2000), who has researched what she termed "self-theories": people's beliefs about themselves, particularly whether they believed that their abilities are innate and immutable ("fixed mindset") or learned and plastic ("growth mindset"). Just as your behavior will change if you have a growth mindset about intelligence, your behavior will change if you have a growth mindset about what else you are capable of. You can become "the kind of person who" does all sorts of things, including having meaningful conversations about equity.

In Chapter 6, we wrote about upending traditional power structures. Leaders are used to being listened to, to being the transmitters of knowledge, decisions, and feedback. Engaging in conversations that center the experience of others entails a reversal in the usual flow of information. Hierarchies have a gradient that may not always be obvious to those at the top; it can be very hard for people with privilege to understand that their perceptions of how easy it is for others to talk to them are skewed. But that knowledge is important in order to make yourself available for honest conversations. As we have emphasized many times, people with power relative to others think that they know more, have better cognitive skills, are better decision-makers and problem-solvers, and are free of the cognitive biases that plague others. It is also known that leaders, even when alerted to their biases, still hold onto them. Further, leaders tend to dominate conversations. They are often the first to speak in groups and speak for the longest time.

In Chapter 5, we discussed the importance of communicating trust and safety in removing some of the barriers to change; people engage in defensive routines when they feel that they are somehow at risk—of being embarrassed, of being judged, of looking incompetent, of being compared with others—there is a fairly long list of feelings that we will defend against. Being skilled at conversation means being able to communicate that the other person is not at risk with you, that it is safe to talk to you. In this chapter we discussed what it takes to do that. We also wrote about what has to happen to support those individual shifts in behavior: the conditions that need to be present that support risk taking and experimentation; the building of perceived self-efficacy; the learning of new knowledge and skills; the feedback and reinforcement. And many, if not all, of those factors are dependent on colleagues and collaborators being able to have conversations with each other.

The best advice for building psychological safety is also the best advice for leadership, coaching, and life in general: Be curious, not judgmental.

AT YOUR DESK OR IN THE HALLS

Reflection Questions

- Some conversations are harder than others. Which conversations do I perceive as difficult and why? How does my focus on comfort impact my willingness to engage in difficult conversations?
- What motivates me to listen? How can I move away from transactional listening?
- How can I get better at conversations? What skills do I need to practice and refine? What is my plan to practice having conversations?

Epilogue

As you will have realized, this is a very personal book. We speak from our own experience, individually and collectively, of years of working to convince educators, mostly leaders, that their colleagues are doing the best they know how to do; that their response to questions and concerns cannot just be labeled as "resistance"; and their requests for clarity cannot be explained away by the adage "change is scary." We have to persuade leaders that their righteous "sense of urgency" is not actually going to be what makes a difference in improving the lives of marginalized students.

We are very optimistic about the potential for using improvement science in service of equity. We have seen how improvement science, as an overall framework and as a set of tools and practices, can be harnessed to improve school and classroom routines and processes in a field that is often replete with hope and vision and rhetoric but lacking in the craft of change. Knowing that change is needed is very different from knowing how to change or what to change to.

We may be devoted fans of improvement science, but that is not where our expertise lies. We aspire to start a conversation about the psychology of change in service of equity because we recognize that to treat issues affecting marginalized students as technical problems to be solved is to wildly underestimate the complexity of humans and change but also to miss the point that we are engaged in a human enterprise, in which our actions today have far-reaching consequences for real people. Those people may be school children now, but they already have aspirations of their own, impactful life experiences, and complicated inner lives. We want the very best for them.

We also have a colossal amount of faith in people. We believe that they have a bottomless capacity for empathy and kindness; that they are highly motivated to feel competent and do the right thing; and that they want to feel respected, connected, valued, and proud of what they do. We believe that there is magic in conversation, that we have this fantastic gift of being able to share with each other what we think and feel in amazing detail and in vivid colors, and that as a result we can change the world.

We hope that you will reach out to us if we can help support you in this work.

Rydell Harrison: rharrison@partnersforel.org
Isobel Stevenson: istevenson@partnersforel.org

References

Abowitz, K. K. (2000). A pragmatist revisioning of resistance theory. *American Educational Research Journal, 37*(4), 877–907.

Argyris, C. (1977). Double loop learning in organizations. *Harvard Business Review, 55*(5), 115–125.

Argyris, C. (1994). Good communication that blocks learning. *Harvard Business Review, 72*(4), 77–85.

Armor, D. J., Conry-Oseguera, P., Cox, M., King, N., McDonnell, L., Pascal, A., Pauly, E., & Zellman, G. (1976). *Analysis of the school preferred reading program in selected Los Angeles minority schools.* Rand Corporation.

Baldwin, J. (1962). As much truth as one can bear. *New York Times Book Review, 14*(2).

Banaji, M. R., & Greenwald, A. G. (2016). *Blindspot: Hidden biases of good people.* Bantam.

Barrett, L. F. (2017). *How emotions are made: The secret life of the brain.* Pan Macmillan.

Beach, J. M. (2021). *Can we measure what matters most?: Why educational accountability metrics lower student learning and demoralize teachers.* Rowman & Littlefield.

Bertrand, M., & Marsh, J. A. (2015). Teachers' sensemaking of data and implications for equity. *American Educational Research Journal, 52*(5), 861–893.

Biag, M., & Sherer, D. (2021). Getting better at getting better: Improvement dispositions in education. *Teachers College Record, 123*(4), 1–42.

Black, P., & Wiliam, D. (1998a). Assessment and classroom learning. *Assessment in Education: Principles, Policy & Practice, 5*(1), 7–74.

Black, P., & Wiliam, D. (1998b). Inside the black box: Raising standards through classroom assessment. *Phi Delta Kappan, 80*(2), 139–144, 146–148.

Bleiberg, J., Brunner, E., Harbatkin, E., Kraft, M. A., & Springer, M. (2021). The effect of teacher evaluation on achievement and attainment: Evidence from statewide reforms. (EdWorkingPaper: 21-496). Retrieved from Annenberg Institute at Brown University. https://doi.org/10.26300/b1ak-r251

Bonilla-Silva, E. (2021). *Racism without racists: Color-blind racism and the persistence of racial inequality in America.* Rowman & Littlefield. 6th edition.

Bryant, A., & Sharer, K. (2021, March). Are you really listening? *Harvard Business Review,* 2–9.

Bryk, A. S., Gomez, L. M., Grunow, A., & LeMahieu, P. G. (2015). *Learning to improve: How America's schools can get better at getting better.* Harvard Education Press.

Bryk, A. S., Greenberg, S., Bertani, A., Sebring, P., Tozer, S. E., & Knowles, T. (2023). *How a city learned to improve its schools.* Harvard Education Press.

Bush-Mecenas, S. (2022). "The business of teaching and learning": Institutionalizing equity in educational organizations through continuous improvement. *American Educational Research Journal, 59*(3), 461–499.

Campbell, D. T. (1979). Assessing the impact of planned social change. *Evaluation and program planning, 2*(1), 67–90.

Carlyle, T. (1841). *On heroes, hero-worship, and the heroic in History.* James Fraser.

Carras, C. (2022, March 21). "Trevor Noah slams media for racist remarks on Ukraine: War 'was Europe's entire thing.'" *Los Angeles Times.*

Chamorro-Premuzic, T. (2019). *Why do so many incompetent men become leaders?: (And how to fix it).* Harvard Business Press.

City, E. A., Elmore, R. F., Fiarman, S. E., & Teitel, L. (2009). *Instructional rounds in education: A network approach to improving teaching and learning.* Harvard Education Press.

Coates, J. (2020). The power elite: A theory of power. *Open Mind, 1*(1), 69–84.

Cochran-Smith, M., & Lytle, S. L. (2009). *Inquiry as stance: Practitioner research for the next generation.* Teachers College Press.

Cohen, G. (2022). *Belonging: The science of creating connection and bridging divides.* W. W. Norton & Company.

Cohen, G., & Sherman, D. (2014). The psychology of change: Self-affirmation and social psychological intervention. *Annual Review of Psychology, 65*, 333–371.

Collins, J. (2001). *Good to great.* Random House.

Collins, P. H. (2022). *Black feminist thought: Knowledge, consciousness, and the politics of empowerment.* 30th anniversary edition. Routledge.

Cooperrider, D., Whitney, D., & Stavros, J. (2008). *Appreciative inquiry handbook: The first in a series of AI workbooks for leaders of change* (Vol. 1). Berrett-Koehler.

Cross, J. R., & Fletcher, K. L. (2009). The challenge of adolescent crowd research: Defining the crowd. *Journal of Youth and Adolescence, 38*(6), 747–764.

Culcea, I. C. (2017). *If it's important it's about me: How subjective importance leads to self-referential attributions* [Doctoral dissertation, State University of New York at Stony Brook].

Datnow, A., & Park, V. (2018). Opening or closing doors for students? Equity and data use in schools. *Journal of Educational Change, 19*(2), 131–152.

Datnow, A., Park, V., & Kennedy-Lewis, B. (2012). High school teachers' use of data to inform instruction. *Journal of Education for Students Placed at Risk, 17*(4), 247–265.

Davidai, S., & Gilovich, T. (2016). The headwinds/tailwinds asymmetry: An availability bias in assessments of barriers and blessings. *Journal of Personality and Social Psychology, 111*(6), 835.

Deming, W. E. (1982). *Out of the crisis.* MIT Press.

Deming, W. E. (2018). *The new economics for industry, government, education* (3rd ed.). MIT Press.

DiAngelo, R. (2018). *White fragility: Why it's so hard for white people to talk about racism.* Beacon Press.

DiMaggio, P. J., & Powell, W. W. (1983). The iron cage revisited: Institutional isomorphism and collective rationality in organizational fields. *American Sociological Review*, 48(2), 147–160.

Doran, G. T. (1981). There's a SMART way to write management's goals and objectives. *Journal of Management Review*, 70, 35–36.

Dweck, C. S. (2000). *Self-theories: Their role in motivation, personality, and development*. Psychology Press.

Dweck, C. S. (2006). *Mindset: The new psychology of success*. Random House.

Eberhardt, J. L. (2019). *Biased: Uncovering the hidden prejudice that shapes what we see, think, and do*. Random House.

Edmondson, A. C. (2012). *Teaming: How organizations learn, innovate, and compete in the knowledge economy*. John Wiley & Sons.

Edmondson, A. C. (2018). *The fearless organization: Creating psychological safety in the workplace for learning, innovation, and growth*. John Wiley & Sons.

Elliot, A. J., & Dweck, C. S. (eds.) (2005). *Handbook of competence and motivation*. Guilford Press.

English, F. W., Fenwick, T., & Parsons, J. (2010). The sustenance of leadership: Exploring the essence of power in principal-supervisor relationships. *Journal of School Leadership*, 20(3), 296–322.

Erikson, E. (1968). *Identity: Youth and crisis*. W. W. Norton & Company.

Eyal, T., Steffel, M., & Epley, N. (2018). Perspective mistaking: Accurately understanding the mind of another requires getting perspective, not taking perspective. *Journal of Personality and Social Psychology*, 114(4), 547–571.

Faulkner, S. L., & Hecht, M. L. (2011). The negotiation of closetable identities: A narrative analysis of lesbian, gay, bisexual, transgendered queer Jewish identity. *Journal of Social and Personal Relationships*, 28(6), 829–847.

Festinger, L. (1957). *A theory of cognitive dissonance*. Stanford University Press.

Fields, B. J., & Fields, K. E. (2012). *Racecraft: The soul of inequality in American life*. Verso Books.

Figlio, D., & Loeb, S. (2011). School accountability. *Handbook of the Economics of Education*, 3, 383–421.

Flyvbjerg, B. (1998). *Rationality and power: Democracy in practice*. University of Chicago Press.

Foucault, M. (1977). *Discipline and punish: The birth of the prison*. Vintage.

Foucault, M. (1980). *Power/knowledge: Selected interviews and other writings, 1972–1977*. Vintage.

Freire, P. (1970). *Pedagogy of the oppressed*. Continuum.

Fullan, M. (2007). *Leading in a culture of change*. John Wiley & Sons.

Garner, B., Thorne, J. K., & Horn, I. S. (2017). Teachers interpreting data for instructional decisions: Where does equity come in? *Journal of Educational Administration*, 55(4), 407–426.

Gilligan, C. (1982). *In a different voice: Psychological theory and women's development*. Harvard University Press.

Goffman, E. (1959). *The Presentation of self in everyday life*. Doubleday.

Goldman, A. (2012). Theory of mind. In E. Margolis, S. Laurence, and S. Stich (Eds.), *Oxford handbook of philosophy and cognitive science* (pp. 402–424). Oxford University Press.

Gould, S. J. (1996). *The mismeasure of man*. W. W. Norton & Company.

Gronn, P. (2002). Distributed leadership as a unit of analysis. *The Leadership Quarterly, 13*(4), 423–451.

Haberman, M. (1991). The pedagogy of poverty versus good teaching. *Phi Delta Kappan, 73*(4), 290–294.

Hariton, E., & Locascio, J. J. (2018). Randomised controlled trials—the gold standard for effectiveness research. *BJOG, 125*(13), 1716. https://doi.org/10.1111/1471-0528.15199

Harrison, R. (2009). Identity, inferiority and social homelessness in adolescent boys. In S. Steinberg & M. Kehler (Eds.), *Boy culture: An encyclopedia*. Greenwood Press.

Harrison, R. (2015). *Uncovering identity negotiation stories of multimarginalized students: Debunking racist and heterosexist hegemonies and developing socially just schools* [Doctoral dissertation, University of North Carolina at Greensboro].

Head, J. (2002). *Working with adolescents: Constructing identity*. Falmer Press.

Heath, C., & Heath, D. (2010. *Switch: How to change things when change is hard*. Crown Business.

Hinnant-Crawford, B. N. (2020). *Improvement science in education: A primer*. Myers Education Press.

hooks, b. (1984). *Feminist theory: From margin to center*. South End Press.

Irby, D. (2022). *Stuck improving: Racial equity and school leadership*. Harvard Education Press.

Johnson, R. S., & La Salle, R. A. (2010). *The wallpaper effect: Data strategies to uncover and eliminate hidden inequities*. Corwin Press.

Kahneman, D. (2011). *Thinking, fast and slow*. Farrar, Straus & Giroux.

Kaplan, R. S., & Norton, D. P. (1996). *The balanced scorecard: Translating strategy into action*. Harvard Business Press.

Kendi, I. X. (2019). *How to be an antiracist*. One World.

Kidd, C., Palmeri, H., & Aslin, R. N. (2013). Rational snacking: Young children's decision-making on the marshmallow task is moderated by beliefs about environmental reliability. *Cognition, 126*(1), 109–114.

Koenig, H., Ames, D., Youssef, N., Oliver, J., Volk, F., Teng, E., Haynes, K., Erickson, Z., Arnold, I., O'Garo, K., & Pearce, M. (2018). Screening for moral injury—The moral injury symptom scale military version short form. *Military Medicine 183*, 11–12.

Kolko, J. (2014). *Well-designed: How to use empathy to create products people love*. Harvard Business Press.

Kristal, A. S., & Santos, L. R. (2021). *G.I. Joe phenomena: Understanding the limits of metacognitive awareness on debiasing* [Working Paper 21-084]. Harvard Business School.

Labaree, D. (1997). Public goods, private goods: The American struggle over educational goals. *American Educational Research Journal, 34*(1), 39–81.

Ladson-Billings, G. (1995). Toward a theory of culturally relevant pedagogy. *American Educational Research Journal, 32*(3), 465–491.

Ladson-Billings, G. (2006). From the achievement gap to the education debt: Understanding achievement in US schools. *Educational Researcher, 35*(7), 3–12.

Langley, G. J., Moen, R. D., Nolan, K. M., Nolan, T. W., Norman, C. L., & Provost, L. P. (2009). *The improvement guide: A practical approach to enhancing organizational performance*. John Wiley & Sons.

Leithwood, K., Harris, A., & Hopkins, D. (2006). Seven strong claims about successful school leadership. *School Leadership & Management, 26*(2), 129–145.

Lewin, K. (1946). Action research and minority problems. *Journal of Social Issues, 2,* 34–46.

Lewis, M. (2004). *Moneyball: The art of winning an unfair game.* W. W. Norton & Company.

Liljedahl, P. (2020). *Building thinking classrooms in mathematics, grades K–12: 14 teaching practices for enhancing learning.* Corwin.

Lindsley, D. H., Brass, D. J., & Thomas, J. B. (1995). Efficacy-performance spirals: A multilevel perspective. *The Academy of Management Review, 20*(3), 645–678.

Longest, K. C. (2009). *Adolescent identity and the transition to young adulthood: Integrating theories, methods, and evidence* [Doctoral dissertation, University of North Carolina at Greensboro].

Lopez, J. L., & Trepal, H. C. (2020). Representation matters: Exploring the underrepresentation of racial/ethnic minorities in higher education leadership. *Journal of Counseling & Development, 98*(2), 161–173.

Lorde, Audre. (1984). *Sister outsider: Essays and speeches.* Crossing Press.

Lowe, L. E. (2012). Testimony in African American worship: The importance of storytelling in the African American church experience. *Journal of Religious & Theological Information, 11*(1–2), 71–84.

Maclean, N. (1992). *Young men and fire.* University of Chicago Press.

Marshall, C., & Oliva, M. (2006). *Leadership for social justice.* Pearson.

McGhee, H. (2022). *The sum of us: What racism costs everyone and how we can prosper together.* One World.

McKoy, S. (2013). *Navigating racialized contexts: The influence of school and family socialization on African American students' racial and educational identity development.* [Doctoral dissertation, University of North Carolina at Greensboro].

Mehrabian, A. (1981). *Silent messages: Implicit communication of emotions and attitudes.* Wadsworth.

Metcalf, H., & Urwick, L. (2003). *Dynamic administration: The collected papers of Mary Parker Follett.* Routledge.

Mischel, W. (1974). Processes in delay of gratification. In L. Berkowitz (Ed.), *Advances in experimental social psychology* (vol. 7, pp. 249–292). Academic Press.

Mischel, W. (2014). *The marshmallow test: Why self-control is the engine of success.* Little, Brown & Company.

Morelli, S., Lieberman, M., & Zaki, J. (2015). The emerging study of positive empathy. *Social and Personality Psychology Compass, 9*(2), 57–68.

Northouse, P. G. (2021). *Leadership: Theory and practice.* Sage Publications.

Okun, T. (2020). White supremacy culture. In D. C. Hilliard III & M. V. Nazaradeh (Eds.), *Uprooting White supremacy in education: Critical literacies for social justice leadership* (pp. 31–50). Teachers College Press.

Okun, T. (2021). *White supremacy culture—Still here.* Retrieved May 27, 2023, from https://drive.google.com/file/d/1XR_7M_9qa64zZ00_JyFVTAjmjVU-uSz8/view?usp=embed_facebook

Oluo, I. (2018). *So you want to talk about race.* Seal Press.

Painter, N. I. (2010). *The history of white people.* W. W. Norton & Company.

Pascale, R. T., Sternin, J., & Sternin, M. (2010). *The power of positive deviance.* Harvard Business Press.

Perkins, D. N., Jay, E., & Tishman, S. (1993). Beyond abilities: A dispositional theory of thinking. *Merrill-Palmer Quarterly, 39*(1), 1–2.

Phillips, E. K. (2019). *The make-or-break year: Solving the dropout crisis one ninth grader at a time.* The New Press.

Pollock, M. (2004). *Colormute: Race talk dilemmas in an American school.* Princeton University Press.

Porath, C. (2015, May 11). The leadership behavior that's most important to employees. *Harvard Business Review.* Retrieved June 8, 2023, from https://hbr .org/2015/05/the-leadership-behavior-thats-most-important-to-employees

Purpel, D. (2000). Goals 2000: The triumph of vulgarity and the legitimation of social injustice. In H. S. Shapiro & D. E. Purpel (Eds.), *Critical social issues in American education: Democracy and meaning in a globalizing world* (pp. 179–190). Erlbaum Associates.

Rogers, E. M. (1995). *Diffusion of innovations.* Simon and Schuster.

Ross, L., & Nisbett, R. E. (2011). *The person and the situation: Perspectives of social psychology.* Pinter & Martin.

Rother, M. (2009). *Toyota kata: Managing people for improvement, adaptiveness, and superior results.* McGraw Hill Education.

Safir, S. (2017). *The listening leader: Creating the conditions for equitable school transformation.* John Wiley & Sons.

Safir, S., & Dugan, J. (2021). *Street data: A next-generation model for equity, pedagogy, and school transformation.* Corwin.

Saini, A. (2019). *Superior: The return of race science.* Beacon Press.

Seijts, G., Latham, G., Tasa, K., & Latham, B. (2004). Goal setting and goal orientation: An integration of two different yet related literatures. *Academy of Management Journal, 47*, 227–240.

Sellers, R. M., Smith, M. A., Shelton, J. N., Rowley, S. A. J., & Chavous, T. M. (1998). Multidimensional model of racial identity: A reconceptualization of African American racial identity. *Personality and Social Psychology Review, 2*, 18–39.

Senge, P. M. (1990). *The fifth discipline: The art and practice of the learning organization.* Doubleday/Currency.

Shapiro, S. (2005). *Losing heart: The moral and spiritual miseducation of America's children.* Lawrence Erlbaum Associates.

Skiba, R. J., Arredondo, M. I., & Williams, N. (2011). More than a pipeline problem: Latino students and disproportionality in school discipline. *Teacher College Record, 113*(2), 285–322.

Skrla, L., Scheurich, J. J., Garcia, J., & Nolly, G. (2004). Equity audits: A practical leadership tool for developing equitable and excellent schools. *Educational Administration Quarterly, 40*(1), 133–161.

Solórzano, D., & Bernal, D. D. (2001). Examining transformational resistance through a critical race and LatCrit theory framework: Chicana and Chicano students in an urban context. *Urban Education, 36*(3), 308–342.

Solórzano, D. G., & Yosso, T. J. (2002). Critical race methodology: Counter-storytelling as an analytical framework for education research. *Qualitative Inquiry, 8*(1), 23–44.

Spillane, J. P. (2006). Distributed leadership. *The Educational Forum, 70*(2), 143–150.

St. Clair, S., Mahr, J., & Schenker, L. (2021, May 21). Chicago vaccines went to many residents of affluent suburbs early on, data shows. *Chicago Tribune*. Retrieved May 27, 2023, from https://www.chicagotribune.com/coronavirus/vaccine /ct-coronavirus-chicago-vaccine-dose-inequity-subrbs-20210521-he7w4kyd7 fdsnhtwtwe3vzxs4e-story.html

Steele, C. (2010). *Whistling Vivaldi: And other clues to how stereotypes affect us.* W. W. Norton & Company.

Stevenson, I. (2019). An improvement plan is not enough—you need a strategy. *Phi Delta Kappan, 100*(6), 60–64.

Stevenson, I., & Weiner, J. M. (2021). *The strategy playbook: Principles and processes.* Routledge.

Stiggins, R., & DuFour, R. (2009). Maximizing the power of formative assessments. *Phi Delta Kappan, 90*(9), 640–644.

Stipek, D. (2005, March 23). "Scientifically based practice": It's about more than improving the quality of research. *Education Week, 33*, 44.

Stogdill, R. M. (1948). Personal factors associated with leadership: A survey of the literature. *The Journal of Psychology: Interdisciplinary and Applied, 25*, 35–71.

Tatum, B. D. (1997). *Why are all the Black kids sitting together in the cafeteria?* Basic Books.

Tokuhama-Espinosa, T. (2018). *Neuromyths: Debunking false ideas about the brain.* W. W. Norton & Company.

Toussaint, J., & Barnas, K. (2021). *Becoming the change: Leadership behavior strategies for continuous improvement in healthcare.* McGraw Hill.

Trope, Y., & Liberman, N. (2010). Construal-level theory of psychological distance. *Psychological Review, 117*(2), 440.

Trzeciak, S., & Mazzarelli, A., (2019). *Compassionomics: The revolutionary scientific evidence that caring makes a difference* (pp. 287–319). Studer Group.

Weick, K. E. (1993). The collapse of sensemaking in organizations: The Mann Gulch disaster. *Administrative Science Quarterly, 38*(4), 628–652.

Weick, K. E. (1995). *Sensemaking in organizations.* Sage.

Weick, K. E. (2007). Drop your tools: On reconfiguring management education. *Journal of Management Education, 31*(1), 5–16.

Weick, K. E., & Roberts, K. H. (1993). Collective mind in organizations: Heedful interrelating on flight decks. *Administrative Science Quarterly*, 357–381.

Welton, A., Owens, D., & Zamani-Gallaher, E. (2018). Anti-racist change: A conceptual framework for educational institutions to take systemic action. *Teachers College Record, 120*(14), 1–22.

Whitaker, B. (1999, April 8). Prosecutor says indictment of Austin schools will help deter test tampering. *The New York Times*, A18.

Wiliam, D. (2011). *Embedded formative assessment.* Solution Tree.

Wilson, A., Almerico, G., Johnston, P., & Ensmann, S. (2020). Examining educational leadership dispositions: A valid and reliable assessment of leadership dispositions. *International Journal of Educational Leadership Preparation, 15*(1), 17–28.

Woulfin, S. L., & Weiner, J. (2019). Triggering change: An investigation of the logics of turnaround leadership. *Education and Urban Society, 51*(2), 222–246.

Yeager, D. S., Purdie-Vaughns, V., Garcia, J., Apfel, N., Brzustoski, P., Master, A., Hessert, W. T., Williams, M. E., & Cohen, G. L. (2014). Breaking the cycle of mistrust: Wise interventions to provide critical feedback across the racial divide. *Journal of Experimental Psychology, 143*(2), 804.

Yoshino, K., & Glasgow, D. (2023). *Say the right thing: How to talk about identity, diversity, and justice.* Simon and Schuster.

Yurkofsky, M., Peterson, A., Mehta, J., Horwitz-Willis, R., & Frumin, K. (2020). Research on continuous improvement: Exploring the complexities of managing educational change. *Review of Research in Education, 44,* 403–433.

Zaki, J., & Ochsner, K. (2012). The neuroscience of empathy: Progress, pitfalls and promise. *Nature Neuroscience, 15,* 675–680.

Zuberi, T. (2001). *Thicker than blood: How racial statistics lie.* University of Minnesota Press.

Zuckerman, M. (1979). Attribution of success and failure revisited, or: The motivational bias is alive and well in attribution theory. *Journal of Personality, 47*(2), 245–287.

Index

Note: Figures are denoted by *f* in the below index.

Ability, 41
Abowitz, K. K., 27
Accountability, 103, 110
    and goals, 83–85
    outcomes-based, 121
    system, 112–113
Achievement gap, 43–44, 62, 87–88,
    98, 111
Action, theory of, 83
Active listening, 34, 131
Adjacent possible, 53–67
    leveraging, 59–66
    positive deviance, 59–62
Advanced Placement (AP) classes, 5
African American, 64
    and same gender loving (SGL), 29
After-school programs, 39
Almerico, G., 41
American schools, 116
Ames, D., 64
Antiracism, 112, 133
Apfel, N., 81
Appreciative inquiry (AI), 62
Argyris, C., 74, 119
Armor, D. J., 80
Arnold, I., 64
Arredondo, M. I., 94
Aslin, R. N., 72
Asset-based approaches, 63
    and intersectional approaches, 49
Assimilation
    and group, 27–28
    and negotiation, 28–29
Attack, 74, 134–135
Attribution theory, 71–73, 117
Audits, equity, 122–123
Austin High School, 114

Baldwin, James, 10
Banaji, M. R., 76

Barnas, K., 135
Barrett, L. F., 33, 135
Batalden, Paul, 12
Beach, J. M., 110
Behavioral norms, 136
Behavioral theories, 41
Belief, 4–5, 14–15, 17, 23, 28, 96–97,
    137–138
    about change and about people,
        69–86
    improvement science, 42–43
    in people, 17
Belonging
    and identity, 13, 20, 23–26
    sense of, 29, 33, 36, 48, 61, 81, 120
    social groups, 26
Below-the-green-line beliefs, 42–43
Bernal, D. D., 27
Bertani, A., 7
Bertrand, M., 117
BHAG. *See* Big Hairy Audacious Goals
    (BHAGs)
Biag, M., 41
Biases, 138
    cognitive, 14
    and psychological distance, 75–77
Big Hairy Audacious Goals (BHAGs),
    84
BIPOC. *See* Black, Indigenous, People
    of Color (BIPOC)
Black, 10, 13, 18, 27, 30, 60, 126
    human rights, 12
Black, Indigenous, People of Color
    (BIPOC), 44–45, 88, 94
Black, P., 73, 110
Black church services, 64
Blame
    game, 94–95
    and infantilization, 93–95
Bleiberg, J., 84

Body composition, 76
Bonilla-Silva, E., 108
Brass, D. J., 80
Brunner, E., 84
Bryant, A., 132
Bryk, A. S., 7, 119
Brzustoski, P., 81
Bubble kids, 3
Bush, George W., 112
Bush-era educational reforms, 112
Bush-Mecenas, S., 7, 12

Campbell's law, 114–115, 115
Carlyle, T., 41
Carnegie summit, 100
Carras, C., 108
Case Western Reserve University, 62
Centering students learning
    vs. student-centered learning, 21–23
Chamorro-Premuzic, T., 14
Characteristics, 42
City, E. A., 115
Climate, 35
Coaching, 45
Coates, J., 91
Cochran-Smith, M., 116, 118
Co-conspirators, 47
Cognitive capacity, 132
Cognitive psychology, 22
Cohen, G., 23, 33, 61, 73, 81
Collaboration, 43
    equity-centered, 47–48
Collaborators. See Co-conspirators
Comfort
    emotional, 127
    privilege of, 126–129
Compliance, focus on, 114
Concept of data
    broadening, 107–123
Condescension, 94
Conflation
    several consequences, 89
Conry-Oseguera, P., 80
Constructivist mindset, 51
Constructivist theories, 22
Contingency theories, 41
Conversations
    about equity, 128, 137
    absolute necessity of, 124–138
    and big ideas, 136–138
    metacognitive, 125, 129
    skills, 129–136
Cooperrider, D., 62

County Attorney Oden, 115
COVID-19 vaccine, 59–60
Cox, M., 80
Crawford, Brandi Hinnant, 37
Critical consciousness
    and Praxis, 46–47
Culcea, I. C., 72
Culturally sustaining pedagogy, 48–49
Culture, 73
Curriculum, 19

Darwin, Charles, 109
Data, 110, 112
    collection, 34
    contaminated by history, 108–109
    hard, 111
    history, 123
    and instruction, 116
    literacy, 43
    policy, 107
Data-driven decision-making, 56–57
Data-informed decision-making, 117
Data teams, 115–117
    on-track performance, 120
    reconfiguring, 117–122
    theory of action for data teams,
        116–117
Datnow, A., 117
Davidai, S., 128
Decision-making
    data-driven, 56–57
    data-informed, 117
Defensive behaviors, 73–74
Defensive reactions, 75
Defensive reasoning, 73
Defensive routines, 73–75
Deficit-based approach, 62
Deficit thinking, 14, 113–114
Deflect, 133–134
Deflection, 134
Deming, W. E., 2, 12, 84, 119, 121
Deny, 134
Dewey, John, 22
DiAngelo, R., 74, 133, 135
DiMaggio, P. J., 91
Discipline
    disparities, 19
    restorative approach, 19
Dispositions
    background on, 40–42
    equity-focused, 45
    of equity leaders in education, 44–45
    in improvement science, 42–43

leadership, 41
liberatory improvers, 45–51
three key elements, 40
Distributed leadership, 104
Doran, George T., 58
DuFour, R., 121
Dugan, J., 7, 32, 34, 35, 107
Dweck, C. S., 73, 78, 138

Eberhardt, J. L., 14
Edmondson, A. C., 14, 85
Education
debt, 111
and empathy interviews, 33–35
and equity, 8–10
equity leaders in, 44–45
inequities, 9, 51
motivation, 82
power structures, 90
reform, 124
student-centered approach, 22
Educational reform, 80
Bush-era, 112
Educators, 7
and equity, 8, 110
and goals, 84
and improvement science, 15
Effort, 78
Egocentrism, 136
Elliot, A. J., 73
Elmore, R. F., 115
Emotional comfort, 127
Emotions, 132
Empathy, 13, 17, 38
in education, 34
interviews, 34–35
and leadership, 39
English, F. W., 88
Ensmann, S., 41
Epley, N., 135
Equitable climate
schools, 35
Equity, 1–2, 43, 54
audits, 122–123
centering, 16
conversations, 125, 128, 130
and education, 8–10
and educators, 8
focused discussions, 121
focused endeavors, 95
and improvement science, 13, 52
meaning, 9
racial bias, 13–14

and racism, 9
zero-sum game, 11
Equity-centered collaboration,
47–48
Equity-focused
dispositions, 45
improvement, 40
leadership, 92
Equity leaders
in education, 44–45
Erickson, Z., 64
Erikson, E., 24–25
ESSA. See Every Student Succeeds Act
(ESSA)
Ethical leadership
and sustainable change, 49–50
Every Student Succeeds Act (ESSA),
109
Experiences, 13, 17–18
current, 18f, 19f
future, 20, 20f, 21f
schooling, 31
Eyal, T., 135

Fenwick, T., 88
Festinger, Leon, 96
Fiarman, S. E., 115
Figlio, D., 83
Fixed mindsets, 138
Flyvbjerg, B., 87
Focus groups, 35–37
Follett, Mary Parker, 103
Foucault, M., 90, 92
Freire, Paulo, 94
Frumin, K., 47

Galton, Francis, 109
Garcia, J., 81, 122
Garner, B., 84
Gilovich, T., 128
Glasgow, D., 133
Goals
and accountability, 83–85
and educators, 84
learning, 84
performance, 84
stretch, 84
Goffman, E., 74
Goldman, A., 33
Gomez, L. M., 7, 119
Good to Great (Collins), 84
Google, 101
Greenberg, S., 7

Greenwald, A. G., 76
Group
    and assimilation, 28
    identity, 26
Growth mindset, 138
Grunow, A., 7, 119

Haberman, M., 113
Hair color
    and women, 76
Harbatkin, E., 84
Hard data, 111
Harris, A., 88
Harrison, R., 26, 29, 30, 32, 33
Harvard University, 92
Haynes, K., 64
Head, J., 24
Heath, C., 60
Heath, D., 60
Hessert, W. T., 81
Hinnant-Crawford, Brandi, 6
Hispanic, 60
A History of White People
    (Painter), 109
Holocaust, 108
Honors Algebra, 134
Hopkins, D., 88
Horn, I. S., 84
Horwitz-Willis, R., 47
Human interactions, 99
Humble, 135

IDEA. See Individuals with Disabilities
    Education Act (IDEA)
Identity, 37, 81
    and belonging, 23–26
    minority, 27
    multiple marginalized, 32
    negotiation, 28–29
    social, 25–26, 28
Ideological legitimization, 91
The Improvement Guide
    (Langley et al.), 2
Improvement habits, 43
Improvement plan
    schools, 72
Improvement Process Map, 3f
Improvement science, 1–2, 6, 104
    and equity, 52
Improvement teams, 63, 104–105,
    120
Improvement theory, 115
Inclination, 40

Inclusive learning environments, 48
Individuals with Disabilities Education
    Act (IDEA), 114
Inequity, 9, 44, 88, 100
    educational, 51
    and inequality, 89
    and inequity, 89
Infantilization
    and blame, 93–95
Institute of Healthcare Improvement,
    12
Institutionalization, 91
Institutional logics
    and mental models, 6–8
Instruction
    and data, 116
Intersectional approaches
    and asset-based approaches, 49
Interviewee
    vs. interviewer, 34
Interviewer
    vs. interviewee, 34
Interviews
    empathy, 34–35
Intrinsic motivation, 82
Irby, D., 11

Jay, E., 40
Johnson, R. S., 107
Johnston, P., 41

Kahneman, D., 132
Kaplan, R. S., 110
Kauffman, Stuart, 53
Kendi, Ibram, 16, 75, 112
Kennedy-Lewis, B., 117
K–12 experiences, 29
Kidd, C., 72
King, Martin Luther, Jr., 53
King, N., 80
Knowledge
    and power, 93
Knowles, T., 7
Koenig, H., 64
Kolko, J., 13
Kraft, M. A., 84
Kristal, A. S., 75

Labaree, D., 114
Ladson-Billings, G., 111, 120
Laggards, 71
Lagging indicators, 115
Langley, G. J., 2

Language, 44, 48, 60, 79, 85, 87
  body, 130 135–136
  informal, 77
La Salle, R. A., 107
Latham, B., 58, 84
Latham, G., 58, 84
Leadership, 39
  dispositions, 41
  distributed, 104
  equity-focused, 92
  trait theory of, 41
  visionary, 56
Learning goals, 84, 85
Leithwood, K., 88
LeMahieu, P. G., 7, 119
Lewin, Kurt, 61
Lewis, M, 135
Liberatory approach, 59
Liberatory improvement science, 105
Liberatory improvers
  and dispositions, 45–51
Liberatory leadership, 97
Liberatory power sharing, 100–105
Liberman, N., 76
Lieberman, M., 33
Liljedahl, P., 73, 115
Lindsley, D. H., 80
Listening
  student, 121
Loeb, S., 83
Longest, K. C., 25
Lorde, Audre, 101
Lytle, S. L., 116, 118

Maclean, Norman, 81
Macroaggressions, 35
Mahr, J., 60
Malnutrition, 59
Mann Gulch disaster, 81
Marginalized group identity, 26–29
Marsh, J. A., 117
Marshall, C., 49
Marshmallow test, 71–72
Master, A., 81
Mazzarelli, A., 35, 36
McDonnell, L., 80
Mehrabian, Albert, 135
Mehta, J., 47
Mental models
  and institutional logics, 6–8
Mentorship, 45
Metacognitive conversation, 125, 129
Metcalf, H., 103

Microaggressions, 35, 92
Mindsets, 77–79, 138
  fixed, 138
  growth, 138
Minority identities, 27
Mischel, W., 71
The Mismeasure of Man (Gould), 109
MMRI. See Multidimensional model of
  racial identity (MMRI)
Moen, R. D., 2
Montana, 81
Montessori, Maria, 22
Morelli, S., 33
Motivation, 82–83
  education, 82
  intrinsic, 82
Multidimensional model of racial
  identity (MMRI), 26
Multiple marginalized identities, 32

NAACP. See National Association
  for the Advancement of Colored
  People (NAACP)
National Association for the
  Advancement of Colored People
  (NAACP), 112
NCLB. See No Child Left Behind
  (NCLB)
Negotiation
  and assimilation, 28–29
  identity, 28
Nichols, Nichelle, 53
Nisbett, R. E., 71
Noah, Trevor, 108
No Child Left Behind (NCLB), 56, 109
Nolan, K. M., 2
Nolan, T. W., 2
Nolly, G., 122
Normalizing offices, 32
Norman, C. L., 2
Northouse, P. G., 89
Norton, D. P., 110

Ochsner, K., 33
O'Garo, K., 64
Okun, T., 56, 90
Oliva, M., 49
Oliver, J., 64
Open-ended questioning, 34
Oppositional social identity, 27
Organizational change, 124
Organizational psychology, 70
Outcomes-based accountability, 121

Painter, Nell Irvin, 108
Palmeri, H., 72
Park, V., 117
Parsons, J., 88
Pascal, A., 80
Pascale, R. T., 59
Patronizing treatment, 94
Pauly, E., 80
Pay attention, 132–133
PDSA. See Plan-do-study-act (PDSA)
   cycles
PDSA Cycles. See Plan-Do Study-Act
   (PDSA)
Pearce, M., 64
Pedagogy
   culturally sustaining, 48–49
Peer coaching program, 73
Perceived self-efficacy (PSE), 78, 80
Perception
   of rightness and power, 92–93
Perkins, D. N., 40
Peterson, A., 47
Phillips, E. K., 114
Piaget, Jean, 22
Pierce, Chester M., 92
Plan-do-study-act (PDSA) cycles, 2,
   54, 85
Polite company, 128
Pollock, M., 75, 127
Poor assumptions
   and unintended consequences,
      112–117
Positive deviance, 59–62
Poverty, 54, 76, 87, 93, 113
Powell, W. W., 91
Power, 88–89, 102, 105
   dynamics, 1
   hoarding, 102
   and knowledge, 93
   power-over, 103
   and perception of rightness, 92–93
   renegotiating, 96–98
   sharing liberatory, 100–105
   structures and education, 90–91
   power-to, 104
   traditional structures, 93
   power-with, 103
Pragmatic action, 46
Pragmatism, 14–16
Praxis
   and critical consciousness, 46–47
Prosocial behavior, 75
Provost, L. P., 2

PSE. See Perceived self-efficacy (PSE)
Psychological distance, 76
   bias and, 75–77
Psychological safety, 85
Psychology, 96
Purdie-Vaughns, V., 81
Purpel, D., 28

Qualitative research method, 36

Racial bias, 13–14, 53
Racial identity, 79
Racism, 65, 72, 75, 90, 109, 112, 134
   conversations about, 125–128
   and equity, 9
   superior, 108
Racist, 3–4
Ramirez, Manny, 87
Rand Corporation study, 80
Rehabilitation Act, 114
Research-based program, 118–119
Resistance, 27
Richards, Ann, 112
Roberts, K. H., 15
Rogers, Carl, 22
Rogers, E. M., 71
Ross, L., 71
Rother, M., 2

Safety, psychological, 138
Safir, S., 7, 13, 32, 34, 57, 107
Saini, A., 108
Same gender loving (SGL), 29
   and African American, 30
Santos, L. R., 75
Schenker, L., 60
Scheurich, J. J., 122
Schools
   American, 116
   equitable climate, 35
   improvement plans, 72, 110
   social justice, 40
Sebring, P., 7
Second World War, 61
Seijts, G., 58, 84
Self-control, 71, 72
Self-determination, 48
Self-efficacy, 13, 17, 66–67, 80, 83, 92
   and stereotype threat, 80–81
Self-protection, 73
Self-questioning, 28
Self-reflection, 28, 51
Self-theories, 79, 138

Senge, P. M., 91, 112
Sense-making theory, 117
Sense of belonging, 29, 33, 35–36, 48,
    61, 81, 120
Sensitivity, 40
Sexual identity, 30, 79
SGL. *See* Same gender loving (SGL)
Shapiro, S., 27
Sherer, D., 41
Sherman, D., 73
Site-based management, 111
Skiba, R. J., 94
Skrla, L., 122
SMART goals, 57–59. *See also* Specific,
    measurable, achievable, relevant,
    and time-bound (SMART) goals
Sneed, Michelle, 38
Social capital, 28
Social cohesion, 34
Social groups, 29–30
    and belonging, 26
Social homelessness, 29–33
Social identity, 25–26, 28, 37
    oppositional, 27
Social justice
    and schools, 40
Social norms, 92
Social order, 95
Social psychology, 70, 72
Social reality, 23
Social structures, 27, 53, 99
Sociology, 96
Solòrzano, D. G., 27, 32
Specific, measurable, achievable,
    relevant, and time-bound
    (SMART) goals, 55
Spillane, J. P., 103
Springer, M., 84
Standardized testing, 56, 93, 107, 112
Star trek, 53, 54
Status quo
    interrogating, 95–96
Stavros, J., 62
St. Clair, S., 60
Steele, C., 80, 127
Steffel, M., 135
Stereotype, 80
Stereotype threat
    and self-efficacy, 80–81
Sternin, J., 59
Sternin, M., 59
Stevenson, I., 2, 120
Stiggins, R., 121

Stogdill, R. M., 41
Story
    power of, 16–17
Storytelling, 64–66
Street data, 57
Strengths-based approach, 62
Stretch goal, 84
Student-centered approaches, 29
Student-centered learning
    vs. centering students learning,
        21–23
Students
    asset-based view, 121
    behavior, 35
    centering experiences, 18–37
    empowerment, 103
    and focus group, 35
    listening, 121
    sense of belonging, 23
    socially homeless, 30–31
    White, 88
Superintendents, 69
Supremacy culture, white, 90
Sustainable change
    and ethical leadership, 49–50
System
    focusing on, 119–121
Systems thinking, 12–13

Tasa, K., 58, 84
Tatum, B. D., 27
Taylorism, 7
Teachers, 35
    empowerment, 118
    self-reflective, 79
Teaching
    and student-centered approaches,
        22
    technical challenge, 116
Technical challenge
    and teaching, 116
Technical work, 15
Teitel, L., 115
Tell stories, 77
Teng, E., 64
Test-based theory of action,
    109–112
Testimony service, 64–65
    lessons learned, 65–66
Thomas, J. B., 80
Thorne, J. K., 84
Time
    as tool of power, 99–100

Tishman, S., 40
Tokuhama-Espinosa, T., 132
Total Quality Control movement, 7
Total quality management (TQM), 111
Toussaint, J., 135
Toyota Kata (Rother), 2
Tozer, S. E., 7
TQM. *See* Total quality management (TQM)
Traditional leadership models, 62
Traditional mental models, 56
    limitation, 55–59
    visionary leadership, 56
Traditional power structures, 88–91
Traditional structures
    power, 93
Traffic barriers, 120
Trait theory, 42
    leadership, 41
Transformative change
    embracing, 98–99
Transformative relationships, 50–51
Trickle-down effect, 114
Trope, Y., 76
Truth regimes, 93
Trzeciak, S., 35, 36

Uhura, 53
Urwick, L., 103

Values, 16–17
Visionary leadership, 56
Volk, F., 64
Vygotsky, Lev, 22

Washington Water Power Company, 58
Weick, K. E., 15, 81
Weiner, J. M., 120
Whitaker, B., 115
White, 18, 27, 88, 129
    racial hierarchy, 108
    students, 88
    supremacy culture, 90
White supremacy culture (WSC), 56, 100–101
Whitney, D., 62
Wiliam, D., 73, 110
Williams, M. E., 81
Williams, N., 94
Wilson, A., 41
Woke ideology, 75
Women, 94, 109, 130
    hair color, 76
    and people of color, 85
Workshops, 74
World War II, 2
WSC. *See* White supremacy culture (WSC)

Yeager, D. S., 81
Yoshino, K., 133
Yosso, T. J., 32
Young Men and Fire (Maclean), 81
Youssef, N., 64
Yurkofsky, M., 47

Zaki, J., 33
Zellman, G., 80
Zero-sum game, 11, 97
Zuckerman, M., 33

About the Authors

Rydell Harrison is a forward-thinking keynote speaker, performer, consultant, and executive leadership coach who partners with school and district leaders to promote diversity, equity, and inclusion and improve outcomes for all students. A career educator and equity advocate, Rydell is the co-founder of Harrison Solutions, LLC, where he works to provide human-centered professional learning experiences that inspire transformational, equitable, and sustainable changes in individuals, organizations, and communities. Drawing from his experience as an activist, music teacher, principal, and superintendent in Connecticut, North Carolina, New York City, and New Jersey, Rydell sheds light on practical ways your organization can operationalize your equity-focused mission and social justice goals.

As a program coordinator with Partners for Educational Leadership (PEL)—a non-profit organization based in Connecticut with a mission to improve teaching and learning, to reduce achievement gaps, and to promote equity in Connecticut schools—Rydell works closely with leaders on high quality instruction, equity, and continuous improvement. He also serves as the family equity liaison for the Guilford, CT, public schools, where he advocates for students, parents, and guardians who feel they have been treated unfairly due to an identity or affiliation to race, ethnicity, gender, gender identity, sexuality, or religion. Currently, Rydell is an adjunct professor in the Educational Leadership & Instructional Technology Department at Central Connecticut State University.

Rydell holds a bachelor of music education degree from Rutgers University and a master of divinity from Duke University. He also holds a master of school administration, a specialist in education, and a doctor of education in school leadership from the University of North Carolina at Greensboro.

Isobel Stevenson has served as a program coordinator and director of organizational learning at Partners for Educational Leadership (PEL). Since joining the PEL team in 2013, Isobel has worked diligently to support educational leaders in their improvement efforts, whether it is their own leadership skills, their strategic plans, equity in their schools and districts, instruction, or building the capacity of others. She worked for 25 years in public education as a teacher but mostly as a school and district leader.

Prior to moving to Connecticut, Isobel was the chief academic officer for a Denver metro area district, where she supervised the instructional program for the district. Before moving to a central office position, Isobel was a principal and a curriculum coordinator, and taught high school special education and social studies. She also served on the AP Committee of the College Board for AP Geography and was a consultant for National Geographic.

Isobel has taught in three different principal preparation programs: University of Denver, San Jose State University, and the University of Connecticut. Isobel holds an undergraduate degree from Oxford University and a master's in special education from the University of Texas at Austin, where she also obtained her principal's license. She has a PhD in human and organizational systems from Fielding Graduate University. She is also a professional certified coach, which enables her to apply the theory and practice of organizational learning, adult learning, and coaching to the work of educational improvement. Isobel's work at the organization includes equity, leadership coaching, and training coaches; strategic planning and improvement; and supporting instructional improvement. Isobel is the co-author of *The Strategy Playbook: Principles and Processes* (Routledge, 2021), *Making Coaching Matter: Leading Continuous Improvement in Schools* (Teachers College Press, 2023), and several articles on leadership and coaching. She also writes *The Coaching Letter*—a newsletter for educational leaders and coaches (https://isobelstevenson.substack.com/).

Printed and bound by CPI Group (UK) Ltd, Croydon, CR0 4YY

16/04/2025